# HOGAN'S
# HOPE

## A DEAF DOG, A COURAGEOUS JOURNEY,
## AND A CHRISTIAN'S FAITH

*Christian Edition*

*Hogan*

# HOGAN'S HOPE

## A DEAF DOG, A COURAGEOUS JOURNEY, AND A CHRISTIAN'S FAITH

*Christian Edition*

Connie Bombaci

# HOGAN'S HOPE
## A DEAF DOG, A COURAGEOUS JOURNEY, AND A CHRISTIAN'S FAITH

*Persons and events during the first eighteen months of Hogan's life have been in part fictionalized and do not represent or depict any actual person, place, or event.*

*Scriptures marked NIV taken from the NEW INTERNATIONAL VERSION (NIV): Scripture taken from THE HOLY BIBLE, NEW INTERNATIONAL VERSION ®. Copyright© 1973, 1978, 1984, 2011 by Biblica, Inc.™. Used by permission of Zondervan*

*Scriptures marked NASB are taken from the NEW AMERICAN STANDARD BIBLE®, ©1995 by The Lockman Foundation. Used by permission.*

*Scriptures marked ERV taken from The Holy Bible, Easy-to-Read Version copyright © 1987, 1999, 2006 Bible League International. Used by permission. All rights reserved*

*Scriptures marked NKJV taken from the NEW KING JAMES VERSION (NKJV): Scripture taken from the NEW KING JAMES VERSION®. Copyright© 1982 by Thomas Nelson, Inc. Used by permission. All rights reserved.*

*iUniverse books may be ordered through booksellers or by contacting:*

*iUniverse*
*1663 Liberty Drive*
*Bloomington, IN 47403*
*www.iuniverse.com*
*1-800-Authors (1-800-288-4677)*

*Because of the dynamic nature of the Internet, any web addresses or links contained in this book may have changed since publication and may no longer be valid. The views expressed in this work are solely those of the author and do not necessarily reflect the views of the publisher, and the publisher hereby disclaims any responsibility for them.*

*Any people depicted in stock imagery provided by Getty Images are models, and such images are being used for illustrative purposes only. Certain stock imagery © Getty Images.*

*ISBN: 978-1-5320-4327-7 (sc)*
*ISBN: 978-1-5320-4335-2 (hc)*
*ISBN: 978-1-5320-4328-4 (e)*

*Library of Congress Control Number: 2018903636*

*Print information available on the last page.*

*iUniverse rev. date: 03/28/2018*

# Contents

April 10, 1992–March 31, 2008

*"Mama's Boy"*

*There are none so deaf than those who refuse to listen.*
(adapted) Mathew Henry, Commentaries, (1708-1710)

*Who have eyes but do not see, who have ears but do not hear*
Jeremiah 5:21b NIV

# Dedication

For my mother, Grace Ann Balestriere, a good and faithful servant
of our Lord
whose example, words, and faith taught me to trust and to serve.

*Trust in the Lord with all your heart*
*and do not lean on your own understanding;*
*in all your ways acknowledge Him,*
*and He will make your paths straight.*
Proverbs 3:5-6 NIV

*[God is the only one who can make the valley of trouble] a doorway*
*of hope.*
Hosea 2:15 ERV

and
For all God's creatures who need acceptance, love, and hope.

*I will not leave you as orphans; I will come to you.*
John 14:18 NIV

# Foreword

*A* *union made in Heaven.*

Connie is one of the sweetest, nicest people I have ever met in my life. Years ago she came to see me with her handsome Dalmatian dog, Hogan, who, like so many Dalmatians, was deaf. Connie loved him as much as anyone could love a dog or a person for that matter. He was indeed a lucky boy to find himself in such a loving home. Connie did not treat Hogan's deafness as a weakness, which of course it is not, but devoted herself to learning to communicate with him using American Sign Language (ASL). This became an all-consuming project and Hogan, being a very intelligent dog, caught on quickly. One of the signs she used was the one for "I love you" (two middle fingers touching the palm of an open hand). Hogan knew the sign and what it meant. He also knew his own name—the first two fingers held together and pointing sideways—signifying "H." And so much more. It was a beautiful thing to see the two of them so closely bonded and understanding each other so perfectly. One problem was that Hogan could not see Connie's signs when he was out of sight—say upstairs. So Connie devised a vibrating collar to communicate with him that dinner was ready and he would come bounding down to get it. All was well in the Bombaci household. Connie and Hogan both learned so much together that she made it a mission to teach other dog owners that their deaf dogs were not stupid when they looked blankly at their owners trying to get some message across—they were just not hearing. Connie tried and succeeded in communicating with so many of them about what could be done to help their dogs understand their silent world via the medium of ASL. She would drive miles to attend gatherings to demonstrate the wonders that she had discovered by working with Hogan and the two of them became celebrities here in the Northeast.

A day came when a problem struck. Connie woke up to find Hogan tearing around the living room floor and then jumping and diving at unseen creatures beneath the floorboards. It was as if there were imaginary rabbits scuttling around the floor and disappearing down imaginary rabbit holes. Connie's first thought—a mouse infestation with mice running around under the floorboards. But, after careful investigation, Connie and her husband found there were no mice. So what had suddenly caused Hogan to behave this way? No one knew. That was when she brought Hogan to see me. I had seen this behavior before, and it is referred to as light and shadow chasing, a canine compulsive disorder. I am certain that deafness predisposes a dog to this visual compulsion—not that it exclusively affects deaf dogs. There's no solution to the deafness, so we had to work with other strategies. More exercise and more mental occupation were high on the list of suggestions I made. Accordingly, Connie built an agility circuit in her backyard and worked with Hogan every day teaching him many new tricks. They both had fun in this endeavor and Hogan gradually improved. I must admit, an anti-compulsive medication helped pave the way for Hogan's turn around.

One day, I was called to the Oprah Winfrey Show and asked if I had any interesting behavior cases to demonstrate. Hogan's case immediately sprung to mind. I asked Connie if she would come to Chicago with Hogan to appear on the show and Connie, true to form, said yes, never wanting to miss an opportunity to demonstrate Hogan the wonder dog and how deafness need not be a great handicap. I flew to the show, but Connie drove from New England to Illinois—because she thought flying would stress her dear boy. I agreed. On the stage, in front of the nation, Hogan and Connie impressed everyone, including Oprah, and the show was a great success. Since that time Connie and I have remained great friends bonded by mutual respect and admiration. I encourage all of you to dive into this wonderful book and learn more about this intrepid pair. It will teach you about the beauty of a perfect relationship between two completely different species and the oneness of life on this planet as well as the power of love and persistence against seemingly stacked odds. Sit! Read! Enjoy!

Dr. Nicholas H. Dodman
Professor Emeritus, Animal Behaviorist
Tufts University, Boston MA

# Endorsements

"As a person who was owned by dogs for many years, it was a pleasure to meet a special creature named Hogan, a beautiful Dalmatian, and completely deaf, as sadly, a number of the breed are. But Hogan's wise and patient companion Connie had taught him American Sign Language! Hogan understood not only his master but a range of commands by anyone skilled in ASL. Remarkably, Connie brought her friend into a much richer, wider fellowship with us humans, and likewise, us with him. I treasure the memory of meeting that very sweet dog."

Dennis Murphy
*Dateline* NBC Correspondent
Winner of five national Emmy awards for excellence in news reporting

"The moment I saw the premise of Hogan's story, I had never wanted to read any book so badly before in my life. . . One of the most emotionally satisfying and enriching books I have ever read!"

Rosie Malezer
Readers' Favorite, Five-Star Review

"Whether you're a dog lover or not, pick up a copy of Connie Bombaci's, *Hogan's Hope* because it shows a better path to improving ourselves and humanity."

Dan Blanchard
Award-winning author, speaker, and educator. President
of Connecticut Authors and Publishers Association

"Hogan was a special and amazing guy, perhaps 'an old soul,' always knowing and guiding the ones he loved to overcome his 'handicap.' I think maybe he taught us about so many things in so many ways."

John Ouellette, D.V.M.
Madison Veterinary Hospital

"To observe and feel the relationship the author had with Hogan and, in fact, with all of her dogs, was something not often seen between human and canine. It was as though Connie could step inside Hogan and know what he was thinking and feeling. Her and Jim's response, in fact, the entire crowd's response, to Hogan running free for the first time ever is a moment that is frozen in time in my memory. Both my husband, Tom, and I knew that they had just given Hogan the gift of a lifetime."

Trina Bianchi
Partner, Injoy Lure Coursing LLC

"There are a lot of dogs. Some are good dogs. Few are great dogs. You have known an epic dog."

Michael Bower
Former Associate Clinical Professor, Department of Psychiatry, Yale
University School of Medicine

# Acknowledgments

With love, I humbly express my appreciation to all those who selflessly offered their gifts and talents in helping me realize my goal of writing *Hogan's Hope*. I marvel at the number of wonderful folks who brought support and encouragement. I praise our Lord for His abounding love and for bringing everyone into my life. His guidance through His Word made it possible for me to tell this very special story.

I am truly thankful to my dear mother, Grace Ann Balestriere, who provided me a lifetime of learning about the love of our Lord and His merciful acceptance. She was my mother, my mentor, and my light in the darkest of times. She helped me start my writing and lent me her insights. Her voice continues although she no longer walks this earth.

My heartfelt thanks go to my family for their abiding faith in my ability to write this book. They include my dear sister Annette Mehan and her husband Ron, who read and offered their points of view. My wonderful granddaughter, Cassandra DiLorenzo, lovingly offered her talents to create my social networks and connections. My son-in-law, Julius Ferrer, provided his photographic expertise in creating my author portrait. My daughter, Heather Ferrer, drew Hogan's portrait and recommended ideas. My great friends, Barbara Chase and Nancy Warner, provided me the encouragement that I needed to keep going and not give up. And, how do I begin to thank my loyal husband, Jim, who listened, listened again, and then listened more? He lovingly offered his suggestions, his enthusiasm, and, most of all, his belief in me. Thank you all for being safe sounding boards.

I am extremely grateful to the medical experts who helped Hogan in so many ways. They are Dr. John Ouellette who freely gave his love and care to Hogan, even learning sign language to create a deeper bond. His diagnostic abilities and healing hands created a special trust and comfort through the years. His lovely wife and partner, Helen, provided that gentle touch and dedication to succeed when so many were skeptical.

Dr. Nicholas Dodman was our anchor and brought contentment back into Hogan's life. His brilliant ability to set the course kept us secure and made it possible for Hogan to realize greater confidence and happiness. I am deeply appreciative of his professional expertise, his uncanny ability to reconnect with Hogan, and his willingness to maintain a lasting friendship. His efforts helped us spread the word that deaf dogs are indeed worthy.

I am deeply indebted to my steadfast friend and editor, Deborah Miles, who agreed over a decade ago to engage with me on my adventure to write. Her expertise is beyond measure, and her belief in my ability persuaded me to move forward and realize my dream to share Hogan's life with the world once more.

D. Margaret Hoffman served as an inspirational guide who reminded me repeatedly that Hogan's life is worth saving. Her proficient proofreading polished my manuscript and made it shine.

Wayne Voltz contributed his support and insightful, faith-filled spirit in verifying and contributing to my Scripture selections.

Susan Hess Procario, my childhood friend, selflessly persevered to recover my cover image so it could reveal the bond and steadfast relationship between Hogan and me. Her astonishing, artistic talent brought together Hogan's and my hearts for everyone to see.

Jane Colton and her two deaf pups, Dotty and Spotty, became internet friends over twenty-three years ago and served as our advocates to champion the cause to save, train, love, and accept our deaf dogs.

There are so many others that I should acknowledge, and I pray that you know who you are because I thank you from the bottom of my heart. In His love, I love you all!

# Part One

# Pain

*You can feel safe because there is hope.*
Job 11:18 ERV

I believe in God and the wonderful gifts that He has given us, especially the gifts of faith, hope, and love. He bestowed life on all of His creatures and gave them the need to find love in a community of family and friends. One of God's magnificent creations had four legs and eventually became known as Hogan. He came into the world in the usual way, but he was anything but typical.

I don't know all of the details of his life before coming to me as a frightened, abused pup. I can only piece together what the first months of his life must have been like and what he must have been thinking and feeling. He must have wanted a warm bed, a full tummy, and a forever home. Mostly, I believe, he wanted to belong to someone who would give him gentle, accepting love.

I would like to share with you his story, as I have seen it, heard about it, or witnessed how Hogan became a hero who gave hope to so many of God's other creatures.

> *Not only so, but we also glory in our sufferings,*
> *because we know that suffering produces perseverance;*
> *perseverance, character; and character, hope.*
> Romans 5:3-4 NIV

# Comings and Goings

*Flowers appear on the earth; the season of singing has come,*
*the cooing of doves is heard in our land.*
Song of Solomon 2:12 NIV

Winter had persisted for so long and had been dreadfully cold, and the warmth of spring seemed as if it might never arrive. But it was now April 10, and the air rustled the new leaves on the trees that surrounded the fenced cages that held the dogs. The grass was turning green while the daffodils and tulips were appearing in the gardens around the house that was perched atop the hill. Springtime brought new life, and Vicki's puppies would soon be arriving. Vicki lay quietly in her cold, steel pen and sniffed the air. Instinctively, she was aware that something was changing. The temperature dropped, and stray snowflakes announced a coming storm. Vicki knew she had to find shelter. She was alone, and she was very cold.

Anna was the breeder's little girl who loved Vicki. But Anna wasn't home, so no one was coming to make sure that Vicki and her new puppies would be safely sheltered inside. Desperate to find cover, Vicki was relieved to discover that a hearty shove with her nose opened the little entrance to her outdoor run and allowed her to escape the wintry blast. Once inside, she pawed some rags into a soft cushion and settled down to await the birth of her puppies.

While the wind whistled and sleet pinged on the tin roof of the dog pen, the puppies were born. One by one nine wet and skinny puppies emerged. The tenth and final pup took much longer. It seemed he was reluctant to leave the safety of his mama's womb to enter an icy, strange, new world. While his brothers and sisters frantically searched for their mother's nipples, the tenth pup was content to snuggle close to the security of her body. She nuzzled him tenderly and then licked him clean. Finally, Vicki rested while all of her babies blissfully suckled.

During the next few weeks, Anna watched the puppies transform from wiggling, wrinkled newborns into soft, playful balls of white fur. Each day  presented a new revelation. First, their eyes opened, and then as if by magic, the black markings that identified them as Dalmatians, began to appear. Anna must have delighted in their antics as they wrestled for position to nurse and chased one another's tails.

Anna loved all ten puppies. However, there was something about the tenth pup that put a smile on her face or a concerned frown on her brow. He was smaller than the others, yet it was more than his size. Her watchful eyes detected that something was different about him, but she couldn't determine what exactly it was. She suspected that Vicki also sensed a difference because she watched over him more closely than she did the others. With maternal nudges of her nose, Vicki often encouraged him to join the other pups at play, but he preferred to remain in the safety of her warmth.

Anna loved cuddling and fussing over the puppies. They made wonderful playmates and were more fun than her lifeless dolls. After they were weaned, she took pleasure in delivering food to them. All of the other puppies went scampering around her feet when Anna came out of the house with their bowls clanging together. They knew the exact moment she came out the back door, except for Number 10. There was no mistaking the loud bang as the old screen door slammed behind her. Nevertheless, when they started to run off, Number 10 took notice and joined in the chase. He seemed hesitant about events around him, and his littermates always responded before he did. As soon as he got any visual cues as to what was occurring, he joined in the romp. It just took him a moment or two. Anna and Vicki were more protective of him, and his favorite places were being nestled with Vicki or cradled by Anna.

Gradually the days became warmer. The days turned into weeks, and the puppies grew not only in size but in the numbers of their spots. Number 10 played with his littermates totally unaware of a looming event. It would not be long before Anna's father put the puppies up for sale, and they would go to new homes. During dinner one evening, Anna's father, Franklin Brown, made the announcement she had dreaded hearing.

"The puppies are almost eight weeks old," Father said in his stern voice. "I think it's time for me to sell them." He was a hard man who didn't take much interest in their upkeep. Puppies were only important to him if he could make a profit from their sale. Anna wanted to keep all her playmates but knew there was no way that would ever happen. She kept silent and secretly prayed that no one would buy her favorite pup, Number 10. The bond between the two had become strong, and there existed a closeness that was undeniable.

The days that followed were busy getting ready for the sale. Franklin placed an advertisement in the local newspaper and cut the grass while Anna and her mother cleaned up the yard from all the winter debris. Anna also accompanied her parents when the puppies were taken to the veterinarian for their initial shots and examinations.

During his exam of Number 10, the vet grimaced and asked, "Does this little guy hear you?" The question didn't come as a complete surprise to Anna. She and Vicki had been protective of him because he was different from the others, but she was horrified to hear the doctor say to her father, "You have to think about what you are going to do with this pup. You won't be able to sell him and, as you must already know, many breeders recommend that deaf puppies be destroyed." Anna's heart sank in her chest, and she was terrified to think that this was a possibility.

During the drive home, Anna fretfully clung to the young pup. Obviously, he didn't understand the reason, but he must have loved being cozied up against her body. He licked her like he wanted to make it all better, kissing

her chin and face with his tiny, puppy tongue. What he didn't know was that Anna just wanted to keep him from being destroyed.

Finally, she dared to ask the question, "Father, what is going to happen to my puppy?" Anna hugged him even closer and whispered, "I think you're worth more than any other puppy *ever*! I love you, and I want to keep you. I can help you, and I promise that I'll always take care of you." Although the pup couldn't hear her words, he felt her loving touch.

Anna's mother swallowed hard before she could whisper into her daughter's ear, "We'll have to pray and hope real hard, Sweetheart." Elizabeth

Brown was already planning some way to convince her husband to allow Anna to keep her puppy.

Everything was in readiness for the puppy sale. Bathed and wearing colored collars, the puppies entertained visitors who came for an inspection. Anna's pup sat a distance away and carefully watched. Although no one had mentioned the problem of his deafness since the visit to the veterinarian, Anna was certain that her parents had discussed the matter when she was not present. She longed to question her mother about it, but she decided it might be best to avoid the issue for the time being.

As the days passed, Vicki anxiously sniffed each person who entered the yard. Anna's heart hurt as she watched sure that Vicki was sad to see her puppies go. Unnoticed by everyone but Anna, however, Vicki tucked Number 10 close to her whenever strangers were present. Eventually, buyers took each of the nine brothers and sisters away to their new homes. Because her father bred the pups for profit, Anna found it extremely difficult to believe that she would be allowed to keep and protect her puppy. But for the time being, Number 10 was still at home, and he was glad to be there with his mother and loving human.

After all the other puppies were sold, Anna feared the moment of truth had arrived. In an attempt to win her father's favor, she spent extra time helping him with chores and errands. One evening while he read the newspaper, she brought him a cup of coffee and took a seat on his footstool.

Finally, she took a deep breath, and with all the courage she could muster, she asked the important question, "Father, will you let me keep my little puppy?" Without pause she continued her pleas, "I'll take care of him and do anything you want me to do! He won't be a bother, honest! You won't even know that he is around and …"

Father slammed down his newspaper. "We can't afford another dog! What with all the food and veterinary bills, it doesn't make sense to spend money on a dog that can't hear and is worthless. My answer is 'No!' We aren't keeping the dog! It can't hear. It's worthless, and I can't even breed him. It's better just to get rid of him now and have him put down."

Anna was devastated and desperately pleaded, "But I love him, and he loves me. I don't want you to take him away. Anything! I'll do anything if you will let me keep him! Please, Father! Please!"

Franklin was an abrasive man who considered himself to be the head of his household and was not accustomed to having his authority challenged in any way. Faced with his wife's rare look of determination, he stopped his tirade and went back to his reading. The unbearable, deafening silence seemed eternal. Anna's mother placed a finger to her lips and motioned for Anna to stay silent. Elizabeth Brown knew her husband and believed that his love for his daughter might win out over Anna's assertive pleas.

Glancing to his wife and then to Anna, Franklin announced sharply, "All right, you may keep the puppy. But... (another long pause) First, you must agree to ALL my rules and conditions. You better listen before you make promises that you can't keep, Anna, because there will be absolutely NO exceptions. And, if you break the rules just once, the dog goes! Is that understood, Anna?"

"Yes, Father! Anything! I promise, truly I do! I'll do anything," Anna fervently replied.

"First, the dog must live outdoors in his pen. I will not tolerate dogs in the house at any time. NO exceptions. You will be fully responsible for his care. You will not neglect your schoolwork or your chores. Your grades must be good, and you must do more chores besides your regular ones because of this dog. It takes a lot of work to take care of a dog. Otherwise, the dog goes. Is that understood?"

"Oh, yes, yes, yes," cried Anna happily. "I'll do anything you say. Thank you, Father!" She ran to her father and hugged him tightly. She kissed him on both cheeks, and then with a jubilant cry, squealed, "Thank you!" Instantly she disappeared out the kitchen door to see Vicki and her pup to tell them the good news. Uncomfortable with Anna's outburst of affection, Anna's father shook his head and went back to his reading and coffee, pretending not to notice his wife's sly smile of approval. Even Franklin had a momentary expression of satisfaction.

Anna knew that her father meant every word of what he said so she went right to work cleaning the cage and making sure there was plenty of water. Food, on the other hand, was getting low in the bin, and she worried that there would not be enough. But Anna's pup was saved, and if he understood the events of that day, Number 10 would feel joy in having a home.

*Number 10's hope was to stay with his loving Anna forever.*

*"For I know the plans I have for you," declares the Lord, "Plans to prosper you and not to harm you, plans to give you hope and a future."*
Jeremiah 29:11 NIV

# The First Year

The summer sun grew warmer, and Number 10 must have loved each new day with great anticipation of playing with Anna. She rushed home from school every afternoon eager to see her puppy. She rolled on the grass and relished his gentle kisses lavished all over her face. Anna had never known such happiness, and she prayed it would last forever. Of course, Anna made sure that she completed her homework and chores before she even thought about playtime. Nothing could go unfinished if the two were to stay together. Father hadn't made an empty threat. She must fulfill the promises she made to him when he agreed to let her keep the puppy. He meant every word.

Every day the puppy grew bigger than the day before. He played more, jumped more, barked more, and he ate more. The food bin emptied faster, and Franklin didn't fill it up as often as he used to. He also began to complain about the pup's barking. "That darn dog is too loud. Quiet him down, Anna. Quiet him down or else!"

Anna fearfully replied, "He is just so excited to play, Father. I'll get my chores done faster, so he doesn't bark as much. Honest, I will." True to her word, Anna did all her chores, certain that this was going to be the happiest summer of her life.

School ended for the year, and Anna was free to remain at home with her puppy. Together, they played in the grass and took long walks along the country roads. While Anna knelt to pick a bouquet for her mother, the puppy chewed on her shoelaces and stalked shadows created by the branches waving in the warm breeze. The puppy liked to chase the movement, and it looked like he was smiling as he pounced on each shadow.

The arrival of nice weather inspired local townspeople to spruce up their homes, and Franklin's carpentry business improved. These jobs required him to be away

from home more than usual, so Anna took it upon herself to do more of the yard work. She weeded the garden and raked up leaves, sticks, and other debris left behind by the storms of winter. The puppy decided that the sticks she had gathered were for him to play with, and he scampered off with them. When Anna pursued him to retrieve the sticks, it became a game that they loved to play.

One sunny afternoon their lives were turned topsy-turvy when a gray van pulled into the yard directly across from the dog cages. Franklin walked over and talked with the scruffy man who drove the vehicle that was crammed with crates. Anna looked puzzled because she didn't know what they were talking about. What she didn't know was that the harmony of their lives was about to be shattered. What appeared at first to be a cordial conversation suddenly deteriorated into an exchange of waving arms and angry faces. Both men strode over to the pens. Watching carefully from the garden, Anna and Number 10 were horrified to see Franklin come out with two of the dogs. He leashed Vicki who struggled to get loose from his tight grip on her collar. He handed her over to this uniformed man, who led the reluctant dogs into the back of his van and drove off. Elizabeth was peering out the kitchen window and buried her face in her apron to hide her tears. Anna wanted to demand why Vicki was taken away. The angry look on her father's face suggested she keep quiet. Frightened, she gathered her pup in her arms and disappeared into the dilapidated tool shed at the back of the garden.

Despite knowing that Number 10 couldn't hear her words, she still whispered into his velvety soft ear, "Don't worry. Nobody is taking you away."

After a while, Elizabeth called out for Anna to come into the house. As Anna put her pup into his pen for the night, he jumped onto his hind legs with his front paws on the hard, metal wire of the cage. He did not want to be left alone. Number 10 loved being with Anna and wanted to go everywhere she went. But Anna's father had set down the law when he said, "No dogs in the house." The pup didn't understand being all alone in the steel pen. New England nights were cool, and he didn't want separation from the warmth of Anna's embrace. Number 10 must have missed his mama, too. The young pup just wanted love, and he wanted to be with Anna.

Dinner for Anna and her parents was uncomfortable that evening. Her parents ate in stony silence, and Anna was too upset to be hungry. She couldn't figure out why this terrible thing had happened, but she hated that the horrible man took Vicki away. Anna was angry with her father for allowing this to happen. She hoped that something would happen for her family to bring Vicki back home again.

That night when her mother came to hear Anna's prayers and tuck her into bed, Anna dared to sob the question that had haunted her, "Mother, why were our dogs taken away?" For what seemed like hours, Anna's mother looked down in silence. She was always straightforward with Anna and could be trusted to be honest, even with answers that were hard to hear.

Slowly and quietly Elizabeth said with a lump in her throat, "Our pups were taken because we aren't able to take care of them anymore. People say that we aren't a good place for the dogs to live."

While Anna didn't like this reply, she could understand. She witnessed for herself how the cages were becoming rundown, and the food bin wasn't being filled as frequently. She had to scrape the bottom to get a meager amount to put in her pup's bowl. But this made her rage inside, and it also made her anger grow toward her father. She knew that he didn't spend time at the kennels anymore, and she knew he didn't care because the dogs weren't making him money. To make matters worse, he didn't make sure that there was enough food. Over time the dogs became dirtier, hungrier, lonelier, and sicker.

The honking of ducks flying south announced the end of summer. Their call along with the gold appearing on the maple leaves served as a reminder that school and autumn activities were about to begin. Number 10 desperately wanted Anna to remain at home with him, but one of the ultimatums her father had stated was that Anna must do well in school.

Number 10 jumped against his cage door after Anna quickly fed him and then ran off for the first day of school. She didn't stay and only briefly patted him on the top of his head. It must have been puzzling to the pup who didn't understand this shift in routine. Sounds weren't a part of his world. He only felt her hand on his head and saw her mouth moving. But Number 10 knew that she was leaving without him. He whimpered hoping that she would come back and anxiously watched as she hurried across the yard. The pup didn't

Connie Bombaci

move from that spot until the school bus completely disappeared from sight. Then he slumped into the corner of his pen to wait.

Number 10 tried to sleep the day away while Anna was gone but found himself pacing back and forth in his small cage during the hours that they used to spend time together playing. When Anna arrived home, she was busy doing homework and running errands, and there was less time to spend together, especially as the days grew shorter. Number 10 was increasingly lonely, and his meals became much smaller.

> *Be still and know that I am God*
> Psalm 46:10a NIV

\* \* \*

The first snowflakes fell silently to the ground, and they glistened in the light reflecting from inside the house. Initially, Number 10 thought they were part of a new game, and he snapped at them trying to catch them in his mouth. The snow was beautiful, but it was merciless. Alone and very cold in his outdoor pen, the young dog ached to have a warm place to snuggle up. But Anna's father was adamant that all dogs had to remain outdoors even in the bitter temperatures. Any efforts to persuade him to change his mind were of no avail and made him horribly irritated.

"You accepted the rules," he would reply icily. "There's absolutely NO discussion." It was becoming a brutal winter, and the snow seemed endless. With the subzero temperatures, barking became Number 10's only way to gain attention. He barked every night because he wanted warmth, food, and love. Dalmatian fur isn't thick like some other breeds, and the cold pierced through his small body like sharp needles. He was still under a year old, but his barking only served to enrage Anna's father who often complained about losing sleep. He referred to the young dog as either "that dumb mutt" or "that worthless hound."

Conditions were miserable. When the barking became incessant throughout the night, Franklin angrily put on his boots, jacket, and hat and went out to the cage to quiet the pleas for help. The flashlight that he used to make his way to the kennels became his weapon of choice to silence the sounds. Number 10 went into the corner as an attempt to escape from his fury. Large red marks covered his white spotted coat as his weight plummeted. His little body's bones began to protrude making the strikes hurt even more.

He cowered in his cage. After all, it wasn't his fault that he was different. When Anna spent time with him, Number 10 stayed close by her side and anticipated her every movement. He knew the difference between playtime and chore time and conducted himself accordingly. Franklin's hatred was evident. The pup was wary of his presence, especially when he carried that steely flashlight. Anna longed to find some way to convince her father that her pup was smart and that with love and encouragement, he would learn to do lots of things.

"Someday," she thought, "when I grow up, I'll have a home of my own. My puppy will live with me, and no one can tell us what to do. I'll let him sleep on my bed and we'll be happy." Suddenly, her thoughts were interrupted by the sound of frantic barking.

"Oh, no!" she whispered, "Don't bark tonight, please!" But, Number 10 was so lonely and cold in his pen during this winter of so many snowstorms. Temperatures reached record-breaking lows as the snow continually fell, and the pup did not intend to be ignored.

It was not long before Anna heard her father's voice furiously call out, "Anna, you better teach that dumb mutt not to bark!" His voice dropped off, but Anna heard the dreadful ultimatum, "or he'll have to go! I won't put up with this barking every night." Anna grew increasingly frightened. She knew she had to make things better or her father would do something terrible again. She knew that the nightly beatings were excruciatingly painful to her puppy.

Number 10 ran back and forth barking wildly. He was cold. He was hungry. He was alone. Anna hated those nights when her father would angrily plod through the mounds of snow dressed in his ominous hat and boots, armed with his flashlight. He would silence the barking until it was reduced to a pitiful wail, and Number 10's blood stained the snow a bright red. What could she possibly do? Taking an enormous risk, she restlessly waited until she heard her father and mother go to bed. When the house became quiet, Anna tiptoed her way along the hallway to the back door. Slowly putting on her down jacket, wrapping a scarf around her neck, and sliding on her boots, she silently slipped out into the darkness. The full moon lit her path to the dog cages. As she unchained the latch to his cage, she bent down with arms wide open. In a single bound Number 10 found himself in her embrace and then inside the warm jacket. It was so very warm.

Anna knew that taking her pup back to the house was not an option. Suddenly, Anna rose and trudged through the drifts of snow. Keeping one arm under the pup's scrawny butt beneath her coat, she bent and picked up a cardboard box that was stashed behind the overflowing trash barrels. She then wedged the box into the corner of the kennel and stuffed her long, fuzzy scarf inside.

"I'm so sorry, but I don't dare take you inside the house with me. Father would never forgive me and would take you away," Anna sobbed. "Stay bundled up in my scarf, and you'll be warmer. Here, I brought a treat for you." Anna had stolen a crust of bread from the pantry before coming to help. It was sweet, and Number 10 gobbled up every crumb.

The pup watched her turn and trudge her way back through the snow to

the house, and he moved to the ice-covered, metal fencing that separated him from his wonderful human. Whimpers didn't call her back, and his little body shivered uncontrollably as he made his way into the new cardboard den.

*Number 10's hope was that his wonderful human would come*
*back and save him from being so cold and hungry.*

*I would hurry to my place of shelter,*
*far from the tempest and storm.*
Psalm 55:8 NIV

*Hear my prayer, Lord, listen to my cry for help;*
*Do not be deaf to my weeping.*
Psalm 39:12a NIV

# Changes

*Oh, that I might have my request,*
*that God would grant what I hope for.*
Job 6:8 NIV

*But now, Lord, what do I look for? My hope is in you.*
Psalm 39:7 NIV

T he endless snowy days began to warm as the sun shifted its position in the sky. Once again the meadow turned green, and the flowers emerged. Buds sprouted on the trees and some flowered while others matured quickly into leaves. Spring had arrived and with it came Number 10's first birthday. He wasn't as cold, but the wounds on his body healed slowly because of the meager supply of good nourishment. Dark brown blotches began to replace the open cuts, and the black and blue bruises lightened. Anna tried to save him food from her plate, but she had to be very careful not to get caught as her father would take the pup away. Franklin considered Number 10 a "waste of good money."

As the days got longer, Number 10 was sure that Anna would have extra time for him. However, increasing numbers of after-school activities kept her from coming home on time. He watched from his cage as the yellow bus rumbled down the road without stopping. But where was Anna? He didn't understand that she was a teenager now, and her friends were progressively more important. Her girlfriends came over to the house to visit more often. They loved playing with the pup and tossing the ball, but it didn't take long until they all went giggling into the house leaving him alone again. Of course,

Anna still loved him, but when she did arrive home, she had her friends over, her homework to get done, her mother to help with dinner, and her chores to finish. To get Anna's attention and have a good time, Number 10 learned to grab the broom's wiry bristles as a new game of play. Anna would laugh which pleased him, so he continued his attacks. But this pastime was short-lived, and after getting a bit of dry kibble, he was once more left alone to wait.

What no one realized was that a neighbor had been watching Number 10 closely over the course of the year when he came for occasional visits. Without fail, he always went over to the pen, and Number 10 loved having someone else coming to see him. The neighbor's face was kind, and his expressions were soft. The young dog sensed that this man had a compassionate heart, and as his hands glided down the dog's body, they must have felt comforting. He was no longer a little puppy, and his legs were getting long as he grew into a youngster. He couldn't fit into anyone's lap anymore, but he tried with great exuberance as he offered his belly for a nice rub.

Summer came and soon left, and the signs of another autumn began to appear once again. Number 10 was the only dog left in the empty, dirty cages. Unlatched gates swung in the breeze and banged against the sides of the pens. Although he couldn't hear the loud noises, he could feel the vibration against his body. The young pup's world was mixed with extreme highs of anticipated love and great lows of fear and abandonment. His world was silent, but he didn't know anything else. He was confused and longed to understand, and the only way to do that was to watch for some cue. What he did understand was that Franklin Brown's touch was terrifying and cruel.

One afternoon while Number 10 waited for Anna to come home and spend time with him, the caring human drove up to the house. Instead of coming to see Number 10 first like he usually did, he went directly inside the house. He held a leash in his left hand. That was puzzling. It didn't take long for him to come back outside with Anna's mother, and they both walked down to the dog's cage. Opening the gate, the man slowly bent down and motioned for Number 10 to come to him. Most other times the young dog would have scampered over to him, but something felt unusual. Anna's mother was there, and because this man was kind before, Number 10 moved timidly toward him. The treat in the man's hand helped to convince him, and he voraciously devoured it.

The leash that the man carried in his hand was clipped onto Number 10's collar, and he was led to a truck. The man gently lifted the pup inside. Unfamiliar to riding in a vehicle, the pup shrank down to the floor between the seat and dashboard, looking up at the ceiling and the windows. Just before the door closed, Anna's mother and the man shared a hug, and she turned to leave. Number 10 must have been puzzled as he fumbled his way up to peer out the rear window. Dust rose from the driveway as they drove away, and he watched Anna's house grow smaller in the distance.

> *Blessed is the one who trusts in the Lord,*
> *And whose hope is in the Lord.*
> Jeremiah 17:7 NKJV

*     *     *

*Kindness is the language which the deaf can hear*
*And the blind can see.*
Mark Twain

When the first rays of sunlight broke into the bedroom, Number 10 woke with a start, surprised to find himself in his own soft bed inside a warm house. He cautiously poked his head up to make sure this was real, and he wanted to immediately explore the whereabouts of those wonderful smells of food. He rounded the corner to the kitchen where the kind man was having breakfast, and he saw his mouth moving as he stooped down to greet Number 10 with a tender scratch under his chin.

"Good morning, little fella. Are you ready for some breakfast?"

The pup yipped with glee as the kind human mixed a bowl of kibble and a moist blend of meats. Number 10 dove into the bowl pushing it all around the slippery floor, cleaning its sides, and making certain that he got every morsel. He couldn't remember having a tummy that was so full. His long tongue licked all around his mouth and atop his nose to get each crumb that clung to his whiskers. Next, they took a leisurely walk around the neighborhood. The happy pup explored every stick and leaf and jumped back when whizzing cars approached.

Then back in the car, they went, and Number 10 fretted about why he wasn't with Anna anymore. Did she miss him? Her father didn't like him, so he wondered if *he* sent him away. Where was he going? Back to Anna? What Number 10 didn't know was that he was confiscated because of the abuse, neglect, lack of nourishment, and dreadful living conditions he had endured. All the dogs were previously taken for the same reasons, and now it was his fate as well.

The car pulled up to a two-story, brick building, and the pup jumped down out of the back as the door opened wide. They were going inside yet another building. Two in two days. Number 10 fearfully and slowly followed the nice man who kept encouraging him with his motions and smiles.

"Come on, good boy," he said. "We're going to find you a good, forever home."

As they entered the tiled lobby, the leash was loosed and the pup was set free to explore the corners of the room. He apprehensively crawled under chairs and timidly put his paws up on the tables piled high with magazines and newspapers. One slid to the floor causing him to retreat with his tail tucked tightly between his legs. He began to tremble and worry more about what was happening.

Meanwhile, the nice man and the woman behind the tall counter, Mrs. Carroll, chatted while organizing paperwork. Finally, Mrs. Carroll picked up the leash and drew Number 10 to her.

"Hi there," she said, "I bet you would like some tasty dog treats and a fresh drink of water, wouldn't you?" While the pup eagerly chomped on the dog bone, she took note of the bruises on his head and body. "Poor thing," she purred. "I think you are well rid of that family!"

After a thorough examination, she walked Number 10 down a corridor of wired cages holding a wide variety of dogs. Spreading a blanket to protect his scrawny body from the concrete floor, she scratched him under his chin and then secured him in one of the empty pens.

*Number 10's hope was that he would feel safe and wouldn't be left alone.*

*Where then is my hope? Who can see any hope for me?*
Job 17:15 NIV

*He will never leave you nor forsake you. Do not be afraid.*
Deuteronomy 31:8 NIV

# Hope

Ａnd this is where I come into the picture as this pup's new mama. I knew that Number 10 was special right from the first moment that I saw him! The look on his face as I peered into his kennel at the humane society conveyed a deep yearning to belong to someone and to be loved. I could tell that he didn't want to be abandoned, thrown away, like too many other animals. He wished for nothing more than to be accepted and taken care of in the shelter of a good home where he would be warm, well fed, and part of his very own family.

I could see in Hogan's eyes that he was a deep thinker. Just as I studied his posture and expressions, he carefully watched every one of my moves, wanting to know who I was and what I was all about. His eyebrows wrinkled as he questioned whether I was going to reach out to him and be his friend or whether I was going to be another person who simply came for a visit and then left him behind. The corners of his mouth turned up into a slight smile in hopes that I would offer him some much-needed comfort and tender affection.

I soon learned that every day was a grand adventure with this special pup who came to live with Jim, me, and our other four-legged family members. My life, like Hogan's, was about to change forever, and we never could predict what each day was going to bring. We just knew that we were going to take one step at a time, together.

> *[Love] always protects, always trusts, always hopes, always perseveres.*
> 1 Corinthians 13:7 NIV

# The Rescue

Mrs. Carroll returned to the office, took a small file card from the top drawer of her desk and dialed a number. After a moment, she spoke into the phone, "Hello, is Connie there? Oh, good. I'm calling to let you know that a gentleman just brought in a dog for placement that might be of interest to you. The pup matches all of the descriptions you outlined to me about size, sex, and age. I must warn you, however, that he is deaf and appears to have been badly mistreated. So, I believe you will want to consider this adoption very carefully."

I never dreamed that the shelter would find a dog for me so quickly, and I was anxious to see him right away. It had taken weeks of persuasion to convince my husband to agree to adopt a playmate for India, our eighteen-month-old, vivacious Black Labrador. I smiled to myself as I recalled how carefully Jim had detailed the requirements as to gender, age, weight, height, and length of coat. He was certain these would present a roadblock in my efforts to locate and adopt a second dog. I chose to dismiss Mrs. Carroll's warning about the animal's deafness and evident abuse as mere professional observations. The dog fits Jim's description in every way. Surely, I theorized, love would take care of everything else. As a precaution, however, I decided not to place any pressure on Jim until he met and evaluated this special pup.

To make the hour drive to the humane society, I left work on time which was quite unusual for me. I itched with impatience, and I also didn't want there to be *any* possibility for someone else to adopt this particular pup. I found a parking space right next to the entrance.

"Oh, what a good omen!" I said aloud as I removed a leash and a bag of dog biscuits from the seat beside me. I hurried inside.

"Hello. I'm Connie Bombaci. I've come to meet the pup you called me about."

Mrs. Carroll looked up from the desk and laughed, "Goodness, you must be really anxious to adopt another dog. You're out of breath." Mrs. Carroll led me along a short corridor to the adjoining building where the animals were housed. We paraded past a series of cages setting off a cacophony of barking from incarcerated dogs begging for attention and freedom. We finally reached the cell that confined Number 10 who sat quietly in the corner. He appeared unimpressed with us and the commotion our presence had created from the other dogs. While I had been forewarned that he was deaf and in poor physical shape, I was totally unprepared for the sickly, emaciated animal that awaited my inspection. The brown eyes that returned my inquisitive stare reflected

deep pools of pain and loneliness. Occasionally, his body shivered, from the pain associated with the massive, reddish-brown splotches and ugly bruises that covered his body. In contrast to the creature's pathetic appearance, I was impressed by the proud, noble way in which he sat and held his head. After studying him for a moment, I slowly opened the door and entered the cage. Disregarding that he was deaf, I squatted on my heels and murmured soft, encouraging words to coax him to me. He watched me curiously for a long moment before taking a few cautious steps toward me. When he had come quite close, I stretched my hand in a gesture of friendship, but the pup cowered from my touch. This response told me that experience had taught him to be wary and avoid anything that might bring pain. I was understanding and calm and did not remove my hand. Instead, I waited patiently for the dog to realize that I meant no harm.

"I think," Mrs. Carroll whispered as if she feared that Number 10 might hear her, "you should carefully consider whether or not you are going to adopt this dog. He is both deaf and malnourished. I doubt if he's even seen the inside of a house, much less acquired any of the training for living indoors." I heard Mrs. Carroll's words, but I already visualized what a nice bath and a rich diet of love and proper nutrition might accomplish for this poor pup. I also felt certain that without my help, he was doomed to be destroyed and that was unacceptable. My demeanor finally convinced the pup to approach my outstretched palm and take a good sniff. With my other hand, I gently began to stroke the underside of his chin. I knew better than to touch the top of his head. At first, he stiffened nervously at my touch, but then sensing no threat, he relaxed and allowed me to slip a leash on and lead him outside the cage.

Back in the office, I addressed Mrs. Carroll, "You explained to me that since this dog is considered a 'special' adoption, the shelter requires that all members of the family be interviewed and that we wait twenty-four hours after our initial meeting. With all that in mind, I want to telephone my husband and ask him to come as soon as he can. Can he bring our Black Lab so we can tell if they'll be compatible?" Mrs. Carroll nodded assent and focused her attention to the papers on the desk, resisting the temptation to offer a further caution. She could tell that my heart had already been captured.

When Jim and India, our Black Lab, arrived, I was walking the deaf pup on the grass in front of the animal shelter. I kept him loosely tethered as he demonstrated no inclination to run or pull away. My apprehension concerning Jim's reaction to this sad-looking specimen proved unfounded. He immediately smiled and reassured me of his sanction with a hug. Reaching into the back of the car, he unclipped India's seatbelt, and she bounded from the car with her usual exuberance. Knowing that a slow introduction of two pups is always best, everyone kept a safe distance as we returned to the building.

Once back inside, Mrs. Carroll suggested that we all go into the large lecture room where everyone could get to know each other. Immediately, the pups' ritualistic sniffing launched a proper introduction of themselves, and then, as if on command, they went simultaneously into the doggy play mode. Success! They romped together as if they were long-lost friends. Jim, Mrs. Carroll, and I had tears streaming down our cheeks.

"Please, Jim," I cried. "Can we please adopt him?"

Without speaking a word, a twinkle in his eye said, "Of course. Do I actually have any other choice?"

The next twenty-four hours seemed eternal. It was the mandatory waiting period that the shelter required for anyone interested in adopting this dog into their family. The authorities wanted to investigate and be absolutely certain that a future home was indeed a good one and a good match. They wanted nothing to serve as a repeat of his former life. Back at home, I couldn't stop thinking about the deaf dog. I knew that communication with anyone, any pup, was essential. Without solid communication to break down any possible barriers, I was sure that our relationship was doomed before it could even get started.

"How do you think we can talk with this pup and have him understand us?" I asked Jim. "I don't want him confused or feeling disconnected from us. I want us to do everything we can to help him." As educators, we instantaneously had the "Ah ha" light bulb go off. We looked at each other and simultaneously declared, "Sign language!" I continued, "We'll use our hands. Deaf children learn signs. I'm sure he can, too."

My concentration at work the next day was difficult as I kept waiting for the phone call from Mrs. Carroll. The day seemed excruciatingly long. It was almost over when the telephone rang. When I heard Mrs. Carroll's words on the other end of the line, I held back an exuberant cheer. I heard, "Connie, you can come get your new pup." Our home, India, Jim, and I met the criteria.

*I hoped that this pup knew that he now had a forever home.*

> *You will surely forget your trouble,*
> *recalling it only as waters gone by.*
> *Life will be brighter than noonday,*
> *and darkness will become like morning.*
> *You will be secure, because there is hope;*
> *You will look about you and take your rest in safety.*
> Job 11:16-18 NIV

*May the stars carry your sadness away,*
*May the flowers fill your heart with beauty,*
*May hope forever wipe away your tears,*
*And, above all, may silence make you strong.*
Native American prayer by Chief Dan George

# A Dream Come True

*But those who hope in the Lord will renew their strength.*
*They will soar on wings like eagles; they will run and*
*not grow weary, they will walk and not be faint.*
Isaiah 40:31 NIV

Seated beside me on the long ride home, I noticed that my new pup took a definite interest in the passing countryside. It seemed as if he were looking for something or someone. His ears were perked up, and his eyes were as wide as silver dollars. It was a rainy day, and I also noticed that he flinched every time a vehicle passed us, sending a spray of water against the windshield and passenger's window. His head comically panned back and forth as his eyes followed the sweeping, windshield wipers.

When we finally arrived home, Jim greeted us at the breezeway door with tasty cookies in his hands. He was already kneeling on the floor and offering the treats to India and our newest family member. A surprise greeted me as well. On the kitchen counter was a paperback book of American Sign Language (ASL). No need to reinvent the wheel and ASL made it possible for others who may know any number of signs to communicate with the deaf dog in the same way. Our family was on a sensational learning adventure together.

We knew that the first thing the deaf pup had to discover was that hands did the talking. So, to get his attention and teach him that hands were how he would hear things, I chose "sit" as his very first word. Sign of "sit," he got a treat when he would sit. Sign of "sit," he got another treat when he would sit again. Practicing went on frequently, and before dinner the next day, he got it! It was in that same twenty-four hours when he learned another word.

He now knew the sign for "cookie." He wasn't the "dumb mutt" that he was called in his former life with the Browns. He was smart. He could learn. He was worthy.

His life became one learning experience after another and was more than the pup could have ever dreamed possible. I smiled as I watched India and her new friend romp around the family room, scattering several small throw rugs in their wake. Jim designed and built this large comfortable post and beam addition to accommodate grandchildren, puppies, and the many, memory-making family gatherings. Its vaulted ceiling and spacious windows provided lots of light and a magnificent view of the garden and woods that surrounded the Shaker-style home. The sliding doors provided access to the outdoor deck that encircled the entire room. This was a room that the pup would grow to love. This spacious area was affectionately referred to as the "barn," because in addition to being comfortable, indestructible, and bright, it simulated living out-of-doors. The pup could enjoy the spectacular views of the outside while being inside a place of warmth and safety, a place he was never permitted to enter before coming here. Relaxed and warm, the deaf pup curled up next to me on the sofa in the center of the barn. Imagine that. He was never inside a home before, and now, not only was he inside, but he was lounging on a soft sofa.

Often, the game of tag between India and her new sibling switched to one of tug-of-war with one of Jim's old work socks that was knotted on both ends. The deep growls that emanated from their throats as they tugged and shook the sock mercilessly were more humorous than threatening. What fun they had. It was late October so we all enjoyed the beauty of seasonal changes and the antics of the squirrels and the birds as they flitted among the tall trees and snacked at the numerous feeders. When the room was darkened at night, we gazed up at the starlit sky through the windows set high in the peaked roof. Ceiling fans circulated the warm air from the wood-burning stove. He was home. He was inside. He was warm.

I asked, "Jim, have you had any thoughts of a good name for our new pup?"

He replied, "I've been thinking about it but can't seem to come up with anything I like."

"Well, I was wondering what you might think of Hogan? It's Native American for lodging or shelter. I want to make him the solemn promise that he will never be without shelter or home again."

"Sounds good to me," Jim stated approvingly.

"Awesome! Now all I have to do is find out how to sign his name and tell him." I quickly began paging through my trusty handbook and methodically read the directions aloud so I would accurately learn his name. "Okay, I sign the letter 'H' with my fingers touching my right temple because the right temple is the place for signing 'boy.' Got it!" With a deep sense of satisfaction, I signed, "Hogan."

"All right, Hogan, you have a name, and we promise that you will never, *ever* be without a loving and sheltering home."

> *A good name is more desirable than great riches.*
> Proverbs 22:1 NIV

\* \* \*

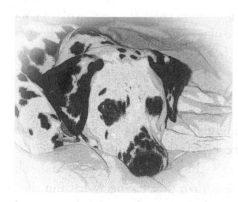

Miraculous events continued for Hogan. Not only did we allow dogs inside the house, but we escorted them upstairs when it was time to settle into bed. Bed. This was a foreign concept to Hogan. Never before had he even imagined a four-posted structure with a fluffy comforter. Still tethered to me, I led him to the side of this king-sized bed and encouraged him to follow India's example of jumping up. Coaxed and cajoled, Hogan seemed fascinated with the idea but hesitant to make a move. Jim hoisted him up, and there he stayed in a deliciously warm and comfy bed with his loving humans.

Jim and I also agreed that a thorough physical checkup for Hogan was imperative. When I called to make the appointment, I asked about having a deaf pup in the family. The technician expressed a bit of concern about the idea, but my mind countered those notions with a total lack of misgiving. I ardently believed that, like humans, everyone is different. And, if a deaf human can learn to communicate and have a quality life, then a deaf pup can as well. No further thought needed.

With the appointment set, we were off to the veterinarian's office the next day. All of Dr. Ouellette's assistants welcomed us warmly and showered Hogan with attention and cookies. We didn't have to wait long until the veterinary assistant ushered us down the hall and into examining room #3.

Hogan quivered nervously. Perhaps the odors of this place were strangely reminiscent, so I cradled Hogan's head in my lap and patted him reassuringly on the sides of his shoulders. As the doctor initiated his assessment by using his experienced fingers to probe my pup's thin, beaten body, my eyes remained riveted on this medical expert's face to catch any reaction. His perpetual smile, however, gave no indication of any possible problems as he struggled with the troubling notion that this young Dalmatian was not altogether unknown to him. Deafness in the breed was not uncommon, and many families just didn't know how to deal with the issue. He decided not to make mention of this quite yet and dismissed the thought as he proceeded to prepare vials for drawing Hogan's blood. Doc usually had his vet technicians assist him when obtaining blood for tests, but because of Hogan's obvious fear, he chose to allow me to hold my new pet. Hogan didn't flinch, so the vet went on to examine the more sensitive areas around his head.

When Dr. Ouellette concluded his examination, he washed his hands

and turned to me with a wry smile. He said, "I suspect that this dog has excellent bloodlines. I also suspect that while he may not have been deliberately starved, he is most certainly suffering the effects of severe malnutrition, dehydration, and exposure. For many reasons, not the least of which is their short coat, Dalmatians are not well suited to living outdoors, especially in extreme conditions. Those conditions are largely responsible for the body sores you see, although there is evidence that he was beaten with something rock hard. As you told me, you are already aware he is deaf, a handicap for which there is no remedy."

Doc continued his explanation that deafness is common in Dalmatians and other breeds with a high level of whiteness. The lack of pigment or whiteness in their skin causes the nerves in the ears to die off during the early weeks of a pup's life. Pigment is essential in the proper working of the nerves in the cochlea of the ears.

"I am amazed that with this handicap and an apparent history of abuse," Doc declared enthusiastically. "he doesn't manifest specific or general signs of a hostile nature. Quite to the contrary, he seems rather gentle and loving. I'm honestly amazed at how well he did." And, after handing Hogan some cookies, he finished, "He's such a good boy."

I nodded assent and continued to stroke the sides of Hogan's neck. Dr. Ouellette continued, "I must warn you that rehabilitation of this pup may not prove to be an easy assignment. If anyone but you, Connie, brought this dog to me, I would probably recommend that they should not attempt. But I've gotten to know you well enough over the years to understand and respect your instincts and devotion to animals. If there is any chance for this dog to find health and happiness, I know it will be in your care. If anyone can take on this challenge, then it's you, my dear."

I smiled, "Thank you, Doc. Thank you!" I had nicknamed him "Doc" many years ago because of his commitment and undeniable love for each and every animal brought to him. Before sending us on our way, he gave us a large bag of vitamins, skin salve, and prescriptive food.

> *A righteous man cares for the needs of his animals.*
> Proverbs 12:10 NIV

\*    \*    \*

Over the next few days, several new rules were put into practice to help boost Hogan's self-confidence and dismiss any potential fear of his new family. First, I hand-fed him all his meals. I would sit in the center of the kitchen floor and hold out my hand brimming with kibble. India got the first bite, and Hogan got the second. I scooped it out of their bowls as fast as they gobbled it down. I am sure that Hogan must have decided that we were good creatures who offered him a forever home, unconditional love, and lots of satisfying food.

The second rule dealt with pups needing to be clean and groomed. Hogan was eighteen months old, and I drew the warm water into my bathtub for his very first bath. I gently lifted him over the sides and into the water that reached the tops of his legs. It must have felt soothing yet unfamiliar to him. As the water poured over his body, his coat became soaked and flattened against his skin. His skeletal frame protruded distinctively, and the ugly, blood-red sores which covered most of his torso and head became painfully visible. I sobbed as I finished his bath and dried him while he sat in my lap. I hugged and rocked him as I held his forehead against my neck.

In addition to being properly groomed, all dogs needed to be well-mannered, especially regarding housetraining. Potty-training habits were in dire need of attention because he had never lived inside a home. Having "taken the position" with his back to me where he couldn't see my arms waving and my hands signing, "NO!" I scooped up and promptly placed Hogan in the backyard. Every hour and immediately following meals, I clipped him to his leash and led him outside to the same area. It became the ritual with me signing, "Potty," every time. Not being able to hear the spoken words, "No," or "Stop," I decided to keep him tethered to me 24/7 and quickly ushered him outside as soon as I detected any indications of his need to go relieve himself. Being tethered was also a protective feature in teaching Hogan what things and places were safe. The greatest benefit of being tethered, however, was that it created a close relationship between my pup and me.

The new rules weren't just for the dogs but were equally important for Jim and me. Good communication was the most important rule, and all of us were learning American Sign Language (ASL). This well-established form of communication was the key to our success, and that pocket-sized handbook went everywhere with us. Out it came whenever I needed a new word to teach Hogan. In fact, I used it with such frequency that it quickly became tattered around the edges and dog-eared on the pages. Hogan grew intent on watching my hands and face for messages which allowed him to live in a world that was no longer totally silent. He was learning, and I was learning rapidly. "Sit," "Cookie," "Come," "Potty," "Eat," and "I love you" were only the beginning. Even India learned the signs, a great tool she could use later in life if her hearing diminished with age.

A startling reaction occurred the first time I signed, "I love you." Hogan immediately shrank to the floor with his ears down, head tucked under, and tail between his legs. I instantly went to the floor and rested next to him for the better part of a half hour. I didn't know the reason for his reaction but suspected that his behavior must be indicative of a dreadful memory. A  quick shift remedied the situation when I used the individual signs for "I," "love," and "you." After a year he learned to tolerate the abbreviated expression for "I love you," just not yet. We both were on a learning curve, and with loving patience, Hogan was destined to zoom ahead.

Some of the rules were good ones to have in place for hearing dogs as well. Jim and I were always mindful of letting Hogan know when we were nearby so he wouldn't be startled or scared. A stomp on the floor or a pat on the bed created a vibration that gave him a signal that someone was present. The expression, "Let sleeping dog lie," didn't originate because of deaf dogs but because of any dog. And, quite frankly, it was a great safety axiom for all dogs. Additional guidelines included approaching slowly from the front where people could be seen and always offering gentle touches to offer reassurances of love.

Positive socialization was another important rule, and both pups strolled the busy downtown sidewalks where people could greet them. Of course, they had to sit politely, and they got biscuits to reward their good behavior. The cars and trucks streamed by on Main Street, and they learned not to be distracted or threatened by their size or sudden movement.

Watching in amusement while the pups played was one of my favorite pastimes. However, I became aware that Hogan's self-confidence was lower than what I preferred. Touching his head must have brought back gruesome memories of his nightly beatings. These images left painful emotional scars. However, Jim's wonderful remedy was gentle, soothing massage that began at the dog's shoulders and, over time, down his sides and into his hips. Finally, after several months, the massage began to include one hand going down his side and the other moving slowly up his neck and onto the top of his head. This calming, daily routine was just a start. It took almost a year before Hogan tolerated head massages.

I established the habit of long, brisk daily walks with our pups. Every morning we all went for our daily constitutional before Jim and I had to leave for our work at school. Venturing out beyond the safe limits of the yard produced great strides in developing Hogan's self-confidence. In addition to a regular training program, Jim constructed a rough-and-ready play yard made with items brought from the shed. At first, it was a simple plank of wood that Hogan jumped over. Then, a plastic barrel with both ends cut off was laid on the ground for him to run through. Every couple of weeks Jim presented another obstacle to learn and achieve. Like a champion, Hogan met each success with applause and treats. It was entertaining to watch him jump for joy and spin about during this increased exercise routine. Every new venture meant that we were needing, learning, and using many more signs. Five, ten, fifteen, twenty, and more. Of course, India was right alongside Hogan showing him exactly what to do.

> *Listen, my son, to your father's instruction*
> *And do not forsake your mother's teaching.*
> Proverbs 1:8 NIV

*   *   *

India and Hogan went everywhere with us. After that first day in his new home, he had experienced a nutritious diet, a safe shelter, a cozy bed with a mixed pack of humans and pups, regular walks, endless play, rubdowns, and hand "talking." And if that weren't enough, Halloween was only a few days away, and a local pet store was holding a costume, picture-taking party. That's all I needed to know.

"Want to go have some fun?" I called out while signing, "Go." India and Hogan were seat belted into Jim's white and blue van and off we went. A long procession of humans and hodgepodge of animals from gerbils to Great Danes greeted us when we arrived at the shop. Most of the animals wore costumes appropriate for the holiday. India wore a jester's collar complete with cap and bells, while Hogan wore a brightly colored, orange scarf. He was not ready for anything to be placed on his head. Both dogs were tethered to us, and we were led to the line. Hogan's first public appearance went fairly well.

While the number of people and animals was daunting, to say the least, I kept him close to my body with reassuring touches to his side and with lots of treats which made most any event a pleasurable experience. There was no limit to the things I wanted him to learn about knowing, be comfortable with experiencing, and be desensitized from fearing.

One surprising obstacle had yet to be overcome, and it was one nobody even imagined existed. The flashlight. We made this horrifying discovery one night when a massive storm took out all the electricity in the area. Without realizing the consequences, Jim went to the kitchen counter's all-purpose drawer and rummaged for the flashlight. Lighting it up provoked Hogan to retreat frantically into the farthest corner that he could find. He scrambled past Jim, over India, and around me almost knocking me down. Old memories must have come streaming back to my poor pup. He must have equated the flashlight with horrible pain. Jim quickly turned it off and looked at me. He attempted to comfort Hogan not realizing that it was the flashlight itself that caused the strong response. It wasn't until he finally put two and two together and got rid of the monstrous light that Hogan began to stop shaking. We sat in the corner for over an hour as Jim gently massaged the pup's body.

This extreme reaction prompted an immediate program of desensitization to eliminate the gripping fear. As the first step, the unlit flashlight was placed on the floor in the farthest corner of the kitchen. Severe trepidation was evident as Hogan walked through the room as far away from that corner as he could. He tucked his tail between his legs, put his ears down, and crouched his entire body. Every few days the flashlight was moved quite literally inch-by-inch until finally, it was in the center of the floor. Next, Jim or I would sit there holding it in one hand with roasted chicken in the other. After weeks of slow movement and patient coaxing, the chicken became much too tantalizing, and Hogan met this challenge. However, the next big test had yet to come and that meant turning the flashlight on.

Once more, we placed the feared tool back under the cabinets in the corner, only this time its light shined across the floorboards. Over the course of several more weeks, we moved it little by little until it was in the middle of the room where it stayed until he didn't seem to notice it was there. Hogan eventually walked through the kitchen stepping directly over it. Conquering the flashlight was a gigantic success, and this scary utensil could now be used to catch his attention from afar. He already loved to chase lights and shadows, so a game was made for him to run after its spotlight. A horrifying fear had now become a playful recreation.

Hogan continued to undergo all kinds of desensitization exercises to address behaviors that included being startled, meeting new dogs and cats, and experiencing a variety of new situations. All of these activities were important and methodically performed. There was only one other time, like the one with the flashlight, that a terrifying scenario presented itself without warning. Everyone was playing in the backyard, and the pups were being run through the playground when a friend of our neighbor walked into the yard. Unfortunately, he was wearing the combination of boots and hat, another terrible reminder of Hogan's pain when Franklin Brown went out to beat him. My pup wildly ran to the back door and ferociously barked as the man continued to approach. Jim politely requested that the man wait until everyone could be settled down. Over time and after patient retraining, our deaf pup appeared to feel safe around the scary items.

The days passed into weeks which turned into months. The humane society where Hogan had been rescued called and announced that they had decided to make a home checkup to evaluate the progress and success of his adoption. The nice man who rescued him from the Browns knocked at the door, and India loudly announced his arrival. Hogan watched her run to the door; then he looked back to me. I called for her to come while Hogan curiously peered around the corner of the kitchen as the man walked down the hallway and into the barn room. He appeared to remember this guy whose scent seemed familiar, and Hogan must have associated it with kindness. As our pup walked towards him, the man sat on the couch and stretched out his hand for it to receive a good sniff and to offer Hogan a cookie from the cookie jar stationed at the front door. Welcoming all visitors became a very positive and joyful affair with the promise of a tasty treat as they entered our home.

"He looks good, Connie, really good." He continued, "He also appears happy in his demeanor and expression. Good living conditions agree with him."

"We are completely in love with this boy. He's made an incredible playmate and sibling for India. They are a perfect match for one another. They wear me out just watching them play together. We couldn't have asked or prayed for more," I nervously chattered.

"I definitely see that he isn't that scrawny pup anymore, and his muscles are becoming quite developed and visible. No more emaciated body. The sores are disappearing as well. In fact, most of them are hardly noticeable at all."

India and Hogan began playing tug-of-war with Jim's knotted sock that proved he was indeed benefiting from the increased nourishment, weight gain, and love. The nice man also became aware Hogan was becoming quite strong and regally handsome. Muscles now rippled on his once skinny hind legs as he tried to best India in a struggle for the almost shredded sock. His coat, now full and shiny, erased all but a few traces of the wounds incurred during his former life. Upon returning to the animal shelter, the humane society's representative gave the director a very positive account of his visit which prompted a story in their next newsletter. Little did I know that this was only the beginning of numerous requests for interviews, news stories, and public appearances.

*Hogan's hope was that this was a never-ending dream come true.*

*When you lie down, you will not be afraid;*
*when you lie down, your sleep will be sweet . . .*
*For the Lord will be at your side.*
Proverbs 3:24,26a NIV

# A Growing Family

*Love one another as I have loved you.*
John 13:34 NIV

It didn't take long before the animal shelter called me at work again. Only this time the staff didn't want to schedule another visit but wanted us to consider adding to our family. It seemed that a petite, four-month-old Dalmatian had been dropped off to be destroyed because she was deaf. The entire staff had become enamored with this little girl whom they dubbed "Face" because of the beautiful, perfectly-placed markings around her eyes and nose. Unlike the other pups who were assigned to their pens unless it was their turn for a walk, Face was permitted to scamper up and down the hallways, slide her way around the slippery office, and escape out into the fenced yard anytime she desired.

"So, Connie, would you be interested in rescuing an adorable, four-month-old puppy who is in desperate need of a loving home?" I was certain that the staff carefully crafted their words as to capture my heart. It worked. My first thoughts were, "Heavens. What is Jim going to say? How am I ever going to convince him to adopt a third dog? It was hard enough getting him to agree to a second one."

"Well," I began, "I honestly don't think my husband is going to agree to this. Oh, my goodness." And then I added sheepishly, "Would you consider letting us foster her until a home can be found? I'd even be willing to help the family with training."

The woman on the other end of the line replied, "In rare situations, we have placed pups in foster care. It hasn't happened very often. But, because of your success with Hogan and the outstanding care given both your pups, I think that we might be able to get that to work in this case. When do you think you can get back to us?" A little pressure never hurt.

I told her that I would call her back the next day after I had the opportunity to talk with Jim. I had to plan what I was going to say, how I was going to convince him, and when the best time to ask would be. Nonetheless, the careful planning went right out the window the moment I saw him.

"Honey, can we please bring home a puppy who will be without a home unless we help? I promise it'll just be until we can find her a home. We can teach her some signs and get her housebroken and…"

Jim interrupted, "Honey, go get her," knowing full well that the moment this little girl walked into our home, she was there to stay. My eyes filled with tears, as I threw my arms around my understanding husband. I made the phone call, and Georgia joined our forever family.

India, Hogan, Georgia, and I were becoming a familiar sight around town. I was passionate about the dogs experiencing the joy of a full life. Their repertoire of words and phrases now included over thirty signs. One of our favorite places to go for a flat-out run was the town green. Of course, Hogan and Georgia were kept on thirty-foot lunge lines while India ran free to catch her beloved Frisbee. It wasn't long before my boy started the game, but he preferred to gallop, running as quickly as possible. Dalmatians were bred to run and that he did well. Freedom to go nonstop with his ears flapping and feeling as if nothing would ever imprison him again was a dream for him, I am sure. Passersby could actually detect the smile on his canine face.

Going for a run became part of our daily routine, and we were often met by folks who had gotten used to seeing us there. One afternoon, a very cordial gentleman approached me while Hogan ran full-steam-ahead at the end of his lunge line. He asked me many questions about having dogs while I continued to throw the Frisbee and hold the leashes.

"How can you handle three dogs at the same time? Why is one off leash and the other two tethered? Do you always use hand signals with your dogs?"

The look of amazement on his face was almost comical when he learned that two of the pups were deaf. I knew that the man hadn't suspected. Why should he? They acted like happy, playful pups. The only difference was that they intently watched my hands and face when I talked to them.

He immediately pulled out a small spiral notebook from his vest pocket along with a pencil and inquired, "May I do a story for our local newspaper?" I motioned for the pups to come, and they settled on the grass to enjoy some recovery time and nibbles. The treats were smaller after such an aerobic workout to prevent upsetting their stomachs. With all but one question answered, the reporter ended by asking, "May I meet you here tomorrow so I can take a picture?"

I was eager to get the word out to the public that handicapped animals, similar to disabled people, could lead useful and fruitful lives. I don't like the term handicapped because I believe that everyone has his or her own personal challenges, some visible and some hidden. Part of accomplishing that mission

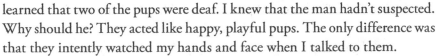

meant that I needed to be unequivocally certain that Hogan and Georgia would be comfortable and confident around large numbers of people. Many social gatherings followed that included parades, street parties, dog walks, and fundraisers. We regularly visited downtown businesses which always required first-rate dog manners. These activities provided tremendous opportunities for humans to learn how to meet and greet, when to ask permission to approach, where to touch, and even how to offer treats to the dogs.

With this increased visibility, it wasn't long before a telephone call came asking about Hogan. To my amazement, the call was from the staff of *Jack Hanna's Animal Adventures*, a nationally broadcast television program. They had read about Hogan and were interested in producing a segment in the episode, "Special People, Special Dogs." My answer was a resounding "yes" to participation, but because I was in a long recovery process from back surgery, the date was put off from summer until mid-December.

Over the course of these months, Hogan continued to learn and flourish in his loving and happy environment. Over thirty of the seventy signs that he eventually learned were now in his repertoire of vocabulary with "Stay," "Jump," "Walk," "Papa," and "I Love You." We constantly made adaptations in our methods of getting the message across. The backdoor light or a flashlight blinking on and off indicated that it was time to come into the house, and the light flickering at the top of the stairway meant to come downstairs. A laser light also caught his attention and led him right to me, and it often became a game of hot pursuit that helped expend some of his limitless energy. I was resolute in my conviction that "A tired dog is a good dog, deaf or not." He appeared to feel safe to run and play all while "hearing" my words.

*Hogan's hope was for continued joy, love, and acceptance.*

*Let love and faithfulness never leave you;*
*Bind them around your neck,*
*Write them on the tablet of your heart.*
Proverbs 3:3 NIV

Connie Bombaci

# Part Three

# Life

Adoption is an amazing gift, and I believe that Hogan adopted us as much, if not more, than we adopted him. Our love was instantaneous, and life became full of possibilities and promise. I was blessed to be able to be a part of this special pup's life and to watch him grasp every day with enormous and energized gusto. His hopes were innumerable as he realized his dream of having a forever family, a full life, and a purpose to make a difference. His delightful personality provided the extra support and encouragement to meet the challenges that came our way and offered the perfect pick-me-up when the untrue myths about deaf dogs seemed to clobber us over the head. Together, we remained steadfast through the tribulations–the bumps in the road. And, while we may have been born of different species, we were connected from the start and shared our hearts. Our desire was for hope to be eternal and for Hogan to experience a life filled with unfettered freedom, unquestionable happiness, and resounding approval.

Changing the world wasn't always easy, but his determined will to beat the odds made a mark for all pups, anyone, with special needs. Hogan took on one challenge at a time, and his successes gave evidence that deafness doesn't have to mean a death sentence. All God's creations are worthy of receiving thoughtful consideration, good treatment, and genuine love. No matter the age, size, characteristics, or type, each is capable of living a wonderful, rewarding life. With the true devotion of the heart, life *is* wonderful, and hope has *no* boundaries.

> *Be strong and take heart, all you who hope in the Lord.*
> Psalm 31:24 NIV

# "Lights, Camera, Action"

> *Make my joy complete by being of the same mind, maintaining*
> *the same love, united in spirit, intent on one purpose.*
> Philippians 2:2 NASB

The big day approached more rapidly than anticipated. We spiffed up the house and groomed all pups to perfection. A pot of soup simmered on the stove while my famous cinnamon coffee cake baked in the oven. The mouthwatering scents wafted through the entire house. We were ready to welcome the renowned celebrity.

We greeted Jack Hanna upon his arrival in our driveway, and he instantly got down on his knees to simultaneously greet all three pups. His face puckered as the pups slathered kisses from his chin to his forehead pushing the front of his hair straight up like the old-style crew cut.

"Boy, Connie, these dogs sure are friendly," he exclaimed with delight. Then he extended his hand to me and said, "Hi, I'm Jack Hanna."

Without a doubt, Mr. Hanna loves animals and extends to them a loving, gentle, and caring hand. He learned in less than a minute how to tell Hogan to "sit," and his response was, "Oh, wow, cool!" He enjoyed his time and joined in all the activities by learning some of the signs, running the playground, and even trying some of the puppy ice cream. He loved it all except for the ice cream! His enthusiasm prompted him to take a heaping spoonful of the frozen treat. When his eyes grew huge, not knowing what to do with this mouthful of not-so-tasty food or where to go, he jumped to his feet turning hilariously back and forth. The entire film crew broke into laughter, barely able to continue filming. The sound tech called out, "Hey, Jack! That's gotta make it into your bloopers tape."

The film shoot continued going along well, and the dogs cooperated by doing everything that the producers wanted. But dogs being dogs, Hogan decided to go off script and started playing with something on the ground. He pranced about the yard with head held high. I then waved my hand above my head to gain his attention and signed, "Drop." When Hogan immediately dropped the badly mangled stick, Mr. Hanna enthusiastically clamored, "I can't get my hearing dog to do that!" I beamed with pride and gave my obedient pup several tasty tidbits from my pocket.

Before wrapping up the day and to further demonstrate how quickly deaf pups can learn, I pulled out a new treat-dispensing toy. It looked like a bright-red bubblegum machine with a long arm that a dog could press down and retrieve bite-sized goodies. Hogan explored its smells and used his paw to hit every part of it trying to gain access to its contents. Suddenly, he hit the jackpot and kibble came pouring out. It took only a few more tries, and he mastered it like a pro. After a round of applause, once again we heard Mr. Hanna's favorite expression, "Cool!"

There were now many requests for us to visit, make presentations, or appear on television programs. Once more, the animal shelter telephoned and asked if we would be willing to serve as the official greeters for their Pet Expo to be held at the city's public arena and civic center. I didn't hesitate to accept the invitation.

We traveled to the event on a bright Saturday morning and greeted many hundreds of people and their pets. The children had a marvelous time learning to use their little fingers to sign and tell our dogs to sit and then give them a cookie. Jim, serving as our careful lookout for any potential problems, caught a glimpse of a nice-looking, young couple standing off to the side. They were watching us and our wonderful interactions with the people entering the exposition. Noticing that the young man was signing to his lovely, female companion, Jim went over to them and invited them to greet the pups. The young woman's eyes lit up, and when she began signing to the dogs, they responded. They understood. Someone besides Jim and me could talk with our pups! A minute hadn't gone by when I looked up at the young man who had tears trickling down his handsome face.

"Never before has my fiancé been able to communicate with a dog. She loves dogs," he said as he tried to hold onto his composure. "We thought that we'd never be able to have a dog of our own."

I offered the young woman Georgia's leash and asked if she would like to spend some time walking around and having some fun with a dog who could understand her. The answer was the sign, "Yes," accompanied by a gigantic smile. Jim stayed close at hand and walked with them as they spent the better part of the morning walking, "talking," and taking pleasure in each other's company.

Sunday morning was another day of meet and greet, and then the dogs went center stage. Equipped with a hands-free microphone, I spoke to a crowd of hundreds and demonstrated how ASL works with deaf pups. The children came up afterward to pet them, sign to them, and give them more treats. However, unquestionably, the best part was that our message about deaf dogs being smart, loving, and worthy was spreading.

*Hogan's hope was that his appearances would spread the news that deaf dogs are worthy of belonging to an understanding and loving community of family and friends.*

*Faith is what makes real the things we hope for.*
*It is proof of what we cannot see.*
Hebrews 11:1 ERV

# The Mission Emphasized

*Hope that is delayed makes you sad,*
*but a wish that comes true fills you with joy.*
Proverbs 13:12 ERV

I adamantly believed that Hogan's story needed to be told, and I became a woman with a mission. The mission was to get the word out to as many people as possible that being hearing-impaired must not sentence an animal to death. A deaf, God-created creature can be a loving, well-trained member of the family. I explained that deaf animals did not need to be destroyed as too many people, including many breeders, believed. My objective was simple. "I want to heighten awareness and educate people that deaf animals can make loving and wonderful members of our families *if* we, as responsible people, remember that they have some special needs. Like any human with a hearing challenge, adaptations can be made."

This mission became especially significant to me after a visit to one of the Dalmatian Club's monthly meetings. After speaking in front of the group of more than thirty people and demonstrating how Hogan followed many ASL words, questions followed one right after the other. Most of the members were hospitable and positive in their remarks. Many of them shared that they honestly were now open to questioning the long-held principle that deaf dogs should be destroyed. While questions and answers were pleasantly exchanged, an underlying feeling of doubt emanated from a visitor seated to the far end of the back row. This skeptical attitude hung like a dark cloud over the room. This person was adamant that "Hogan is an exception to the rule," and went on to say, "He can hear. He has selective hearing." I felt disappointed but said nothing.

During the drive home, I asked Jim what he thought of my presentation and the meeting. "Connie, I know you want to convince everyone that deaf dogs can learn and don't need to be put down. But it's just not going to happen. You need to focus on the ones who did open their eyes tonight and are at least thinking about not getting rid of deaf puppies. I have no question that you made a difference. You did. Don't doubt yourself. Besides, you can only do so much." Jim's words gave encouragement, but I wanted to do it all. I wanted to convince the world that deaf pups are worthy.

*Hope hides in His promises when it seems that few give us grace.*
Unknown

\*     \*     \*

While India, Hogan, Georgia, Jim, and I all continued learning signs, following directions, and playing with great enthusiasm, recollections of the club's meeting haunted my thoughts. I watched the pups to detect the slightest hint of hearing. What better way to receive definite verification of how well, if at all, Hogan and Georgia might be able to hear than to have them tested? Our veterinarian, Dr. Ouellette, recommended that we contact Tufts University Animal Hospital and consult with their well-respected experts. And this is exactly what we did.

The trip to Foster Hospital for Small Animals which is part of Cummings Veterinary Medical Center at Tufts University in Massachusetts was a two-hour drive from our home in Connecticut, but that was of no consequence to me. We arrived and proceeded directly to the crowded lobby which bustled with canines and felines of all shapes, sizes, and colors. Their owners were trying to maintain order over their excited pets. When our name was called to check in, we approached the registration desk where a soft-spoken woman who seemed oblivious to the noise and activity going on greeted us. She gave me paperwork to fill out, issued medical cards, and politely asked us to wait in our seats until our appointment. Being deaf does have its advantages in situations like this as the clamor had no impact on Hogan and Georgia's behavior. Their focus on my hands remained the priority, but sights and smells were most interesting to their other sharpened senses.

When our names were announced, the four of us obediently followed the veterinary technician into a small room full of machines and monitors. The tall, thin doctor was carefully reading the forms I had filled out and periodically glanced up over her glasses to ask questions for clarification. Because Georgia captured the hearts of the technician and doctor with her less intimidating size and sweet face, she got to go first. She was hoisted up onto the stainless steel examining table located in the center of the room. She offered kisses to both the doctor and technician.

As the veterinarian began an overall assessment of Georgia, she asked questions which included, "Does she respond to any sounds at all?" "Does she startle with clanging or if objects are dropped?" "Does she mind being touched in the slightest way?" The corresponding responses were, "No," "Not at all," and "She loves being touched and begs for as much touching as she can get. In fact, if you stop touching her, she relentlessly nudges you until she gets more." As the doctor was performing her preliminary examination of Georgia's petite frame, her technician began untangling an entwined bunch of long wires with what appeared to be probes at their ends. One by one she meticulously placed them on the equipment stand. In between tiny kisses, the doctor attached the probes to Georgia's forehead, around the perimeter of her head, and at the backs of her ears. The last instruments were fed down inside the canals of her ears to get as close to the eardrum as possible. The trick, quite literally, was to keep Georgia from shaking her head. While it took some convincing, the doctor permitted me to cradle Georgia's face in the palms of my hands and maintain eye-to-eye contact with her. After a kiss on her wet, black nose, Georgia remained perfectly still.

A series of signals were sent to the probes, and the results were recorded on a machine that resembled a cardiac monitor. Lines were drawn on paper and sent to the monitor for readings and evaluations. Symbols of Xs, Os, and arrows of different colors were used to gather the information, as pitch and loudness from high to low were recorded. This data gave the experts the big picture. Simply stated, this audiogram graphed what Georgia did and did not hear, and the results verifying that she was indeed deaf. The recurring flat lines indicated that her eardrums did not respond in the normal range of hearing. They did reveal, however, that she had some high-frequency hearing.

Hogan was next, and the doctor studied him with great apprehension. He was strikingly larger and more poised than Georgia. My training, playing, and exercising him had paid off, and he proudly sat next to me. "Has this dog ever bitten anyone?" the doctor asked. "Has he ever demonstrated aggressive behavior?"

"Never," I answered with Jim nodding his head in agreement. "Hogan lets me do anything to him including brushing, even scaling his teeth, trimming his nails, and playing in his food bowl while he eats." My concern rose, so I asked, "Is there a reason you are asking?"

The doctor's reply seemed prejudicial, but I understood that a bias existed against deaf dogs. She added, "I've experienced deaf dogs that will bite under these circumstances."

I offered assistance. "If you let me work with Hogan, I promise that he will behave and permit you to perform the tests." That said, Georgia jumped down off the examination table, and Jim lifted Hogan up onto its cold, metal surface. It was slippery, but with me standing directly in front of him signing "down," "stay," and "calm," Hogan laid down while the probes were set into place. His eyebrows crumpled while his deep brown eyes looked back and forth, up and down. But he didn't move a single muscle.

The doctor appeared astonished. With surprise in her voice, she stated, "I never experienced a dog, let alone a deaf one, who is so well-behaved or obedient, especially since probes are uncomfortably set into their ears. They're usually more nervous and jittery." She added, "I haven't ever seen anyone use American Sign Language with a deaf dog before or witnessed such a tight bond between a master and their dog." The key for us had always been communication. But while Hogan's behavior was spot on, the tests were quite the opposite. There was absolutely no hearing of any kind at any range or at any pitch. The audiogram recorded a completely flat line. Many people would feel sorry for him, but why? Silence was his world, and he never knew a world with sound. He didn't know that he was missing out. He understood and "heard" his family with ASL, body language, and, most importantly, love. As far as he was concerned, everything was perfect now that he had his forever family!

We returned to our home, and as soon as the seatbelts were unhooked, the dogs bounded out to run and play after the tedious hours of travel and testing. Their favorite game of tug-of-war ensued with Georgia smack in the middle. She always seemed to claim this spot, perhaps to never lose. She certainly wasn't the powerhouse that could begin to win the sport over India and Hogan. The pups often seemed to let her think that she had won by dropping their ends. She would prance around the perimeter of the yard lifting the filthy, knotted rope above her head as if it were a prize worth more than anything that she could imagine. I would clap and dance about to congratulate them for playing so nicely, and each received individual and enthusiastic praise. India was first, Georgia was second, and Hogan was third. He was always last, and it made for an expected order within our beloved pack of humans and pups.

The pups could always trust that they would receive quality time and attention. Days included regular walks and aerobic exercise. Constant training was an integral part of every one of our activities. Good manners and obedience skills were requisite. All of it was fun, and except for when Jim and I had to go to work, it was blissful. The warm relationship was based on a steadfast feeling of devotion.

I want so much for people to see beyond their deafness. Deaf dogs do not need to be destroyed because of the incorrect assumptions and myths that plague them. They can and do learn, and they make loving family members when given the proper attention and understanding. Just like a deaf person, we make adaptations. The negative myths are untrue.

Requests for our appearances continued to increase with newspaper articles, write-ups in local town distributions, public cable network shows, and television news coverage's making Hogan and Georgia celebrities. Visits to schools and Sunday school classes heightened awareness, and we gained attention as far away as Japan when we were interviewed twice during radio talk shows. Opportunities came to us out of curiosity, in addition to genuine interest about deaf dogs and how they could be trained, especially using ASL.

*Hogan's hope was that people would realize
the myths about deaf dogs were untrue.*

*Keep your tongue from evil
and your lips from speaking lies.*
Psalm 34:13 NIV

*We want each of you to show this same diligence to the very end,
in order to make your hope sure.*
Hebrews 6:11 NIV

# An Unforeseen Challenge

*But as for you, be strong and do not give up,*
*for your work will be rewarded.*
2 Chronicles 15:7 NIV

*Then you will know the truth,*
*And the truth will set you free.*
John 8:32 NIV

In the midst of our fun and Hogan's growth in stature and confidence, I had to undergo major back surgery. I was gone for more than three days, and the dogs had no idea where I went. Jim could tell that Hogan was anxious as he paced and whined, prodding him to get me. When I arrived home, I inched my way along the front pathway of our home. Unfortunately, my walker got in the way of getting up close to Hogan so I could give him a proper greeting. He wanted desperately to lean his body into me and feel my comforting hands on him. Confused, he backed off and waited, tilting his head side to side. He ran in front of me and came to an abrupt stop next to my chair in the barn room. He was hoping that I would soon be able to pet and reassure him that I wasn't going away again. He didn't like being separated from his rescuer and provider. And, if I wasn't right nearby him, how could he protect me and keep a close watch?

Jim guided me directly to a new, overstuffed recliner and removed my walker so that Hogan had a chance to move in. I was quiet, but I let my right arm dangle over the side of the chair so the tips of my fingers could scratch the top of his head. There wasn't much strength, but my touch gave him relief that I had returned home. Of course, India and Georgia wanted in on the action of being next to me. India intuitively remained subdued and settled herself on the left side of the chair while Georgia crawled under the raised leg portion and buried herself in her private, miniature den.

Days passed, and I remained in my recliner day and night. Nurses and attendants came during the day to lend assistance while Jim was at work teaching. Jim had fenced our yard with an invisible fencing system so that the pups could be let out safely to go potty and play, and as always, India served as the dependable leader. When she was called, she instinctively knew to let Hogan and Georgia know that it was time to go back inside. She would run over to them and give a hard poke to their sides. Most of the time the dogs chose to fall into line because choosing not to listen to her brought a brusque warning or benign peck directly next to their ears.

We were blessed with two wonderful neighbors and friends who came to help take care of the pups. Frankie was a handsome and happy teenager who adored dogs. Daily he came by to take Hogan for an afternoon hike, play a game of fetch, go for a trek around the block, or engage in another extra-exhausting activity. His curly, brown hair accentuated his gleaming eyes and beaming smile, and his caring heart put a perfect exclamation point on their time together. Rita, on the other hand, was the jovial senior who lived directly across the street and brought the dogs mouthwatering leftovers from her family's suppers. Her jacket pockets ballooned with these delicacies, and every inch of her body shook joyously at the sight of Hogan bouncing in circles in front of her until told to "sit."

Life couldn't get any better for Hogan. He had a shelter to live in, food to keep his stomach satisfied, pups to play with, and his human with him twenty-four hours a day, seven days a week. Things stayed this way for the better part of seven months until I was healed. By then I began walking, my strength increased, and I started back to work teaching television production on a part-time basis. The four hours that I was gone didn't seem so bad for the pups who slept much of the time. Little did the dogs realize that soon I was going to be away on a full schedule of eight hours. No one could have predicted that Hogan's anxiety of being alone and abandoned would slowly creep in, robbing him of his newly learned confidence and comfort.

At first, he paced a bit. Then, he seemed more easily distracted by lights and shadows that only he could see. Finally, he began a digging action on the floor and in the yard. Without warning, he would dart at top speed to a corner of the room or a spot on the lawn as if he saw an invisible mouse. He would dig or paw at the ground in what appeared to be an effort to find his imaginary critter. Nothing I tried to stop him worked and the intensity of his behavior grew until I became desperate for a solution. I made an appointment with Dr. Ouellette, who became upset knowing that something was awry. A complete physical examination with full blood work revealed that Hogan was in perfect health.

"What do I do?" I inquired.

"If I were you, I'd take my pup to Tufts again. I read about an animal behaviorist who is well-regarded and just might be able to figure out what's going on with this fine fellow." Dr. Ouellette was rubbing the sides of Hogan's head, as he had grown incredibly fond of him and wanted only "the best of the best." On his own, he had learned some ASL to talk with Hogan and even had laminated sheets with diagrams of the most important words placed in each of his three examination rooms. He encouraged his entire staff to learn them which could prove to be essential if ever there were a situation when I couldn't be there to assist. "Let me make a call and see if I can find out more information that can help you," he continued. "Don't worry, Connie. We'll figure this out. You've come this far already. It'll be fine. I'll let you know who to contact." Less than twenty-four hours later the telephone rang. Sure enough, Doc came through and had the relevant information for me to make an appointment. Dr. Nicholas Dodman, the renowned animal behaviorist at Tufts University, was able to schedule us almost immediately. I was thrilled and relieved, and I believed that Hogan was going to get the remedy he needed to feel better. Help was on the way.

Dr. Dodman personally returned my call the next day. His genteel English accent and his engaging manner of speaking touched my heart immediately, and he gained my confidence. He asked all sorts of questions about Hogan's size, age, breed, background, recent events, patterns of behavior, our daily routine, work schedule, socialization, diet, treats, exercise, and even sleeping habits. By the time the conversation was over, our entire life story was revealed to this wonderful and thoughtful man on the other end of the telephone line.

He stated, "This is quite an intriguing case, Mrs. Bombaci, and I am looking forward to meeting you and your special pup. Might you be able to come within the week?"

By this time, Jim had gotten me an older, white Jeep with the license plate PUPPYZ specifically for transporting the pups. He wanted the four-wheel drive to provide safety during snow storms, and he wanted generous space for three pups to travel comfortably. Having the rear passenger seat collapsed gave the dogs the area they needed to be able to lay down without being cramped. On this particular trip, there was just Hogan who had the entire back to himself. We navigated the two-hour trip along the highways through Connecticut and Massachusetts, enjoying the spring scenery and observing signs of new life.

Once we arrived at the small animal hospital, we proceeded to walk across the front lawn dotted with tall trees. We continued our stroll back up the side paths flanking the kennels. Our legs felt good as they stretched after the long ride, and Hogan's nose enjoyed the hundreds of new scents. The receptionist at the registration desk recorded our names, and within moments Dr. Nicholas Dodman came out to greet us. He looked exactly how I had imagined—tall and slim, with perfect posture and an enchanting face. He wore a white medical coat with his name stitched across the left pocket, in case I hadn't already recognized his amiable manner and distinct English accent. An instant rapport began to develop as he greeted us with an immediate handshake. His attentive eyes met Hogan's with a look of profound desire to explore the pup's personality. His intent to help was evident and genuine. Hogan instantaneously took a liking to Dr. Dodman, and he was eager to follow him to his office and examining room.

We took seats in the room which was a bit crowded with all of us, and Hogan sat in his usual place next to me. Dr. Dodman asked additional questions about my special pup's background and reviewed in detail the information that he had gathered during the initial telephone conversation. He continually watched Hogan.

Then came Hogan's first big test. I had to let him off his leash, which was his lifeline to me. Much to everyone's surprise he continued to sit quite still. He looked intently at everything in the room, particularly at items that moved or shined and caught his eye.

The second test came. Jim and I were asked to exit the room leaving Hogan behind with Dr. Dodman. I later learned that for the first minute or two he stood right where he was and appeared unaffected by the change. However, he just couldn't contain himself a second longer and then began to pace back and forth at the door, bending his front legs low enough to allow him to sniff at the small crack at the bottom. As he relentlessly continued to seek a way back to me, he scratched at the polished tile floor. Maybe he wanted out. Maybe he wanted to get where I was. Maybe? After ten minutes Dr. Dodman summoned Jim and me back into the room and described his observations. With intuitive judgment, he plotted out a course of treatment to alleviate Hogan's compulsive behavior.

To begin, Hogan needed more vigorous exercise added to his daily walks and lunges on the long line. "A tired dog is a good dog," was the perfect adage in this situation. Next, Dr. Dodman recommended that Jim construct additional obstacles in the dog's play yard so that our anxious pup would continue to develop more self-confidence. And, while Hogan knew over thirty signs in ASL when he first met Dr. Dodman, the doctor saw just how smart this pup was and wanted communication ramped up even more. These instructions meant that we needed to learn and teach Hogan as many signs as possible.

Hogan also needed a cue from me to stop when he started his pace-paw ritual. I was instructed to make a big, red placard approximately ten inches by fourteen inches with the letter "H" on it. The second that Hogan started his compulsive behavior, I was to hold this sign up and leave the room as soon as he took notice of it. If he stopped and followed me, he was rewarded with a wholesome, homemade treat.

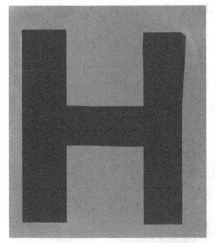

Hogan already benefited from a nutritious diet, but it was modified to one with less protein and no artificial ingredients. He also had to "work" for any treat he was given. Work meant performing tasks that could include "Come," "Sit," "Shake," "Spin," or "Lay down." Lastly, because his brain's chemistry needed some support until this gripping behavior could be conquered, Hogan was temporarily placed on Elavil to help him refocus and become less anxious, especially when he was away from me. Dr. Dodman affectionately dubbed him my "Velcro dog," and I believed him to be spot-on in all aspects of his evaluations.

It took time, but that didn't matter to Dr. Dodman or me. Both of us made the promise to stick by Hogan. We firmly believed in the pup and never gave up hope. With attention, direction, and love, together we battled through the nine months that it took to detect a reduction in his compulsion. He became a happier, more balanced dog, and his pace-paw behavior went down to a level where it was practically extinct. Only under extreme duress did it resurface, but that was rare. The positive belief in Hogan's worth and ability paid off.

I promised to continue to check in monthly with Dr. Dodman to provide updates and afford him the ability to make modifications to our working plan. Visits to see him allowed him the opportunity to observe and monitor Hogan's progress. Furthermore, because of such great progress, he slowly weaned Hogan off the medication. All other portions of the plan, however, remained firmly intact. Both Dr. Dodman and I were tremendously proud of my incredible pup's achievements, and the good doctor consequently included him in his newest book, *Dogs Behaving Badly, An A-to-Z Guide to Understanding & Curing Behavioral Problems for Dogs*. Hogan was one of his indisputable success stories and the epitome of triumph over adversity. For this reason, Dr. Dodman asked if we could be his companions on the *Oprah Winfrey Show* (1996).

Our daughter, Heather (Hogan's human sister as I used to tease her), insisted on driving us to Chicago so our precious pup would not be subjected to the hardships of flying. Heather worked with animals and observed firsthand the effects of being shipped in an aircraft's baggage compartment, and she cared far too much to risk the slightest possibility of him being endangered in any way. Consequently, Jim, who didn't want to chance this grueling expedition with an older car, rented us a nice, oversized sedan with spacious leg room.  The rear seat was all Hogan's to drape across and snooze away our twenty-four-hour road trip.

As we passed the roadside sign, "Welcome to Chicago," I waved my arms over my head and performed a front-seat jig while Heather yelled out, "Whoo hoo!" I spun around to face Hogan and clapped my hands to tell him how happy I was. He always became animated whenever I clapped for him, and I think he knew this signaled that things were good. That seemed to make him happy as well.

We arrived and checked into the hotel suites arranged for us by the HARPO Studios. Heather had hers, and Hogan had his. I had none and jokingly said to Heather, "Well, I guess Hogan will share his with me." Yep! The suite was registered to Hogan Bombaci. I don't think that many pups can claim that they had their own hotel suites.

After an early night, we woke at dawn to give Hogan a last-minute bath, tooth brushing, and nail filing. I wanted him to look immaculately groomed and handsome for the millions of viewers who would see the show. When the limousine pulled up to the entrance of the hotel's lobby, the valet announced, "Hogan Bombaci's limousine is ready." Wow! Again, for a dog. Not for Heather and not for me, but for the pup. The chauffeur was cheerful, and he took elaborate measures to ensure that the canine seat belt was attached properly before attempting to hook our celebrity pup into place. Heather and I merely went along for the ride. Hogan looked regal and sat straight up in his luxurious leather seat as we drove through the streets of the windy city. The fine breeding and bloodlines that Dr. Ouellette had previously mentioned now revealed themselves in the pup's rehabilitated health, reformed behavior, and reinforced self-confidence.

The guests for the show's taping waited in the green rooms where there were makeup artists, hair stylists, and wardrobe specialists checking to guarantee that everyone looked their best and had microphones in place. One of them approached Hogan with some white powder, but because of his miraculous transformation, not a single touchup was necessary. His coat was flawless. It was Dr. Dodman and me who needed primping before appearing on the show.

Hogan was perfectly behaved on and off stage. The lights didn't distract him, and the large audience of unfamiliar faces didn't intimidate him. He followed every request that I signed to him during the on-camera discussion about his deafness, ability to learn sign language, and hard work in overcoming anxiety. Dr. Dodman also elaborated with his respected knowledge of animal psychology.

During a commercial break, Oprah, who was sitting on the stage floor within arm's reach of Hogan, happened to hit her hand hard against its surface. He rotated his head and repositioned his body to look directly at her. She was taken aback, and her eyes opened wide.

"He felt that didn't he?" she exclaimed.

I was beaming with pride, and Dr. Dodman looked like a proud professor. I'm sure that Hogan felt like his star pupil.

We exited the stage when our interview was over and waited in the wings of the studio at the request of the floor manager. Some of the audience members asked to make our acquaintance, and we were more than happy to visit with them. After the tapings of the regular show and a commercial for the Chicago Bulls basketball team were complete, a couple of dozen folks came by for us to meet and greet. Several had questions. Others wanted to pose for a picture with Hogan, and still others just wanted to pet his head. We were delighted that he didn't mind being touched on his head anymore.

Oprah, being her usual, gracious self, came over to us and offered her heartfelt appreciation for visiting her show. I inquired, "May I ask you a special favor?"

Oprah responded instantly, "I know; you'd like a picture of me with Hogan. Right? Not with you, but with Hogan." How perceptive!

*Hogan's hope was for greater awareness and understanding that would create a world of support, solutions, and success for all God's creations.*

*Finally, all of you, live in harmony with one another; be sympathetic, love as brothers, be compassionate and humble.*
I Peter 3:8 NIV

# First Family Vacation

It felt good to be home again. Hogan played with India and Georgia like there was no tomorrow. He barreled at top speed and mastered his play-yard obstacles like a champ. He loved his new life.

Spring had arrived, and Jim and I began making plans for summer vacation. During my recovery, I watched *Animal Planet* almost exclusively and learned about Camp Gone to the Dogs in Vermont. While Jim claimed that he wasn't "a dog person," he loved the pups and did most everything I asked of him. How could anyone argue with that? He allowed me to adopt three pups, snuggled in bed with us at night, built a puppy play yard, and helped take care of them when I couldn't. These were only a few examples of his affection for the dogs. A whole bunch of love lay underneath his sometimes gruff exterior. In reality, Jim was a big softy, and he wasn't fooling anyone except himself. He pretended to protest at first about going to a dog camp, but I appealed to his love of sports by explaining that most of the activities were designed to be athletic. That did the trick. He agreed to give it a go.

I made the telephone call to Honey Loring, the director of the camp, who provided all the pertinent information. Honey was excited to meet us. The deal was as good as closed. The only thing left to do was get our paperwork in order and submitted.

The middle of June arrived, school was out for the summer, and we packed the van with doggie supplies, toys, and luggage. Jim shook his head in amazement with the amount of stuff I wanted to take. Of course, he really wasn't surprised. He knew me, and he knew how much I cherished our pups. My excitement brought a smile to his face as he watched me preparing for the week-long excursion.

The camp was well organized and held at a private school in Vermont. The Green Mountains provided the perfect backdrop where campers and their dogs gathered for a week of fun. The dining hall, dormitories, and staff cabins were in a row with 150 acres of pastures stretching their length. A clear pond glistening in the midday sun offered the promise of a swim for both pups and humans. The pathway led off to the right toward the large, red barn where a crew was working to ready the grounds for the field events. A tent was erected for large group gatherings, lectures, and activities, while smaller tents spotted the grounds to provide shade from the afternoon sun. Flyball boxes and runways were set up in the area farthest to the left for dogs to compete in the speed of retrieval. To the far right, a large selection of "toys" was constructed for the dogs to be trained in safely maneuvering the various levels of agility courses. The venue was without a doubt a doggie amusement park and dream vacation for the most passionate of dog lovers.

At first glance, it all seemed to be organized chaos. Dogs ran back and forth in the field on the left while others tugged on their leashes and owners' arms as they impatiently exited their parked vehicles. Some people were carefully setting up crates and exercise pens, referred to as X-pens, under the trees on the front lawn, while others embraced each other upon their yearly reunion. Over a hundred pepped-up people and almost twice that number of four-legged family members moved about like checkers on a giant game board. The dogs ranged in age from ten weeks to seventeen years and varied in size from toy breeds to mammoth 175 pounders. They were from "best in show" to the "American designer dog" and from being bought at top dollar to rescued off the street. Each one of them, however, was spoiled and especially treasured.

I am usually ready to jump in with both feet, but I was overcome by a sense of uncertainty. I was hesitant to meet other people and their pups straightaway. Instead, I walked my pups near the 500-foot entrance and assessed the activity. I had done all the research and preparation for this doggie vacation, so Jim looked to me for guidance. His face gave the impression of understanding, and he seemed quite content following my lead.

An extensive list of events offered activities ranging from rigorous training scheduled during the cooler morning and evening hours, to more leisurely afternoon hikes, swimming, and classes on topics such as grooming and cooking for the dogs. The mid-day break afforded pups and humans the opportunity to cool down and recuperate from the earlier strenuous activities. The packed schedule offered something for everyone.

"I know we say 'Do it all or just sit around, kiss your dog, and eat bonbons!' But, don't try to do it all if your dog is telling you otherwise," urged the director, Honey, during her welcome under the big tent. "You'll find yourselves dog-tired, and your dogs stressed out. We don't want grumpy campers or sick pups. We're here to have a blast. And, if you aren't conscientious in watching for symptoms of fatigue or overdoing it, you won't be able to continue in the merriment. Remember, if it isn't fun for your dog, don't do it. All of us at Camp Gone to the Dogs want to have another successful year fulfilling our camp's motto, 'A Tail Wagging Good Time!'"

Everyone dispersed to finish settling in. After we registered and received our packet that outlined each day's schedule, we headed back to our camper at the local campsite five miles down the road. We decided to use our little weekender instead of squeezing into a small dormitory room. This way, all our paraphernalia was in one place. An added bonus was that it provided us breathing space away from the multitude of pups who were champing at the bit.

Monday morning was our first full day of camp, and we rolled out of our beds ready to get the festivities underway. The camp provided meals for the two-legged campers, and the first thing Jim and I did was head to the dining hall for some coffee and breakfast. Since dogs were not allowed into the cafeteria during mealtimes, they were relegated to their crates that were under the trees less than 100 feet away.

As we made our way along the path to breakfast, we noticed a group of dogs barking and lunging at the end of their leashes while their handlers struggled to maintain their hold. A crowd of campers stood or sat on the grassy slope in front of the cafeteria. They surveyed the immense field below and cheered for the dog who was barreling full throttle after what appeared to be a plain, white plastic bag. The bag was being pulled from one end of the massive field to the other, crisscrossing its way back to the start point with an energized pup striving to catch its white "prey" in its jaws. Just when the dog got to the finish, the bag stopped, and the handler scooped up his pup who was trying to catch the prize. I wasn't sure who was more fun to watch, the pup or the human. The dog didn't want to give up shaking and shredding the bag, and the owner desperately tried to gain control of the pup so the next dog in line could have a turn in this game nicknamed "running the bunny." This was lure coursing at its best, and it grabbed our complete attention.

A husband and wife team, Tom and Trina, ran this operation. They set it up during the coolest parts of the day, early morning before breakfast and late evening after dinner. The dogs exerted an enormous amount of energy which made the threat of becoming dangerously overheated a critical consideration. This game stimulated the dogs' instinct to pursue prey. In this case. the prey was a white plastic bag, affectionately dubbed "the bunny." A series of pulleys were positioned from one end of the field to the other with a sturdy line of string pulled from pulley to pulley in a pattern that simulated the path of an escaping rabbit. This continuous line began and ended at the start/finish line and looped around a wheel powered by a small motor.

It looked like enormous fun, and I was certain that all three of our pups would have a grand time playing this new sport. But Hogan and Georgia couldn't be off leash because they couldn't hear the call of "come" if their backs were turned towards me. Furthermore, when they were off leash, such as during agility, they could always see me and were close enough for me to snatch up the strap attached to their collars. Each morning and evening we would all stand on the sidelines watching and cheering on the pup who was focused on capturing the prey. Hogan barked more than he ever had, and I was sure he wanted to chase that bunny down and across the meadow.

The schedule for each day at camp offered a long list of choices including herding, tracking, flyball, obedience, jump chute, and agility. Our first pick of the week was the beginner's agility course training. I was eager to learn about this event because how hard could it be? Jim had already crafted makeshift obstacles for Hogan to play on at home. Now there was a much greater variety of equipment that provided bigger jumps, walkways, shoots, A-frames, weave poles, and even a seesaw. The instructor was a reputable expert in the fields of agility and training, so Hogan was going to learn from the best. She was a skilled professional who was adept and totally devoted to her specialty.

Jim and India became our own team number one while Hogan and I became number two, and together we walked across the field to sign up for class. We waited excitedly, yet patiently, in line. I was intent on Hogan doing well, so I scrutinized every team as they made their way through each new object. I hadn't yet told anyone that Hogan couldn't hear because it didn't seem to be of great  consequence. However, when the instructor wanted me to take him off leash or stand in locations for various obstacles where he wouldn't be able to see me, I had no other choice than to disclose his deafness. The teacher's face changed, which said it all. She followed up, "I've never had a good encounter with a deaf dog, so I don't want to let you down. Honestly, I don't know how well you're going to do. I also want you to keep him on his regular leash rather than the shorter, training strap."

I understood her reservations, but I envisioned this as a brand-new quest. Plus, it was only the beginning of the week. I wanted nothing more than for Hogan to do well and take advantage of as much training as possible. Therefore, I complied with every one of the teacher's requests and her directions on how to learn the various pieces of equipment. Hogan mastered one obstacle at a time and then went on to put two, three, four, and more together as the week went on. He loved agility, and other campers took notice and commented on his eye-catching happiness as he triumphantly performed new jumps, walkways, and hoops. His deafness intrigued the other participants, and people began to take expressed interest in his performance.

By the end of the week when class members were coursing as many as six obstacles on a run, Hogan took off like a whiz as soon as I signed, "Go."

He followed every sign. The instructor looked extremely pleased. When we got to the front of the line, she was different than on our first day. It was as if a light bulb was clicked on, and she began to brainstorm ideas that would help Hogan and me communicate and navigate the course with greater precision. Because he had proceeded so well, she suggested that Hogan graduate to wearing the shorter strap instead of his six-foot leash. This way I could let go of him without losing the ability to snatch him up if necessary. Each successful pass brought accolades and treats. A job well done deserves lots of rewards. At the end of the hour-long classes, this wonderful instructor always shared a warm hug. I wasn't sure who was thanking whom or who learned the most during those sixty-minute sessions. Hogan and I happily bounced our way back across the field feeling victorious about our accomplishments.

When a class was over, India and Hogan would go into their crates for a much-needed rest while Georgia got her chance to take on the agility hurdles. She did well, but she didn't do as well as Hogan! The wonderful instructor was ready for her and offered many clever suggestions on how to attack the course.

*Everyone* had a success story, and that's what camp was all about. Jim was thrilled for us and became excited about Hogan's progress. He jumped into all the activities that I chose during the week, especially the athletic ones.

Mary, the tracking instructor, was kind, insightful, and compassionate. While she sometimes seemed reserved, on occasion, she could be very animated. She laughed with her whole body until even Hogan could feel her infectious joy. She was fired up about his participation in her tracking class and confident that he would do well. She reminded us, "Because of his deafness, Connie, he depends more on his other senses which, I am sure, have become more powerfully keen." She was right, and Hogan put his nose to the ground and sniffed his way to the target. Mary became one of his cheerleaders from the starting block and urged us to hold back on nothing that our remarkable pup liked.

Hogan also excelled in flyball where he got to use his skill to push down on things with his paw. His treat machine had taught him well. Folks always

cheered for him when he returned with such exuberance to the finish line, and his enthusiasm became contagious to other campers and their pups. When they saw a deaf dog performing successfully, they tried even harder to master the particular skill.

Hogan's performance was stellar in every class we attended. He came when called during the recall class. He strutted his stuff when he dressed up for the costume party, spun during freestyle, and retrieved the hot dog without eating it. He even learned how to do some tricks that included finding the ball in the three-cup shuffle.

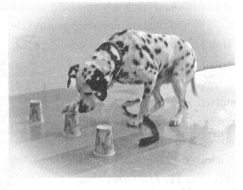

However, Jim and I continued to watch dogs dashing on the lure course and yearned for Hogan to have a shot at this exhilarating sport. We stood on the sidelines while Hogan barked ceaselessly and bounced up and down. He craved a piece of the action.

"Jim, do you think we could let him try this?" I asked. "You could stand at the far end of the field just in case he tried to keep going."

Jim shook his head with hesitancy when he replied, "I don't know. He could get a head start on me and then he'd be gone."

"I could ask some of the other campers to help out. What do you think?"

Trina was a kind woman who partnered with her husband to make this opportunity available to the campers. While she stood at only five-feet in height, her heart was "bigger than all outdoors," and she offered it to anyone who earnestly loved their pets. What Jim and I didn't know was that she had been watching us from her post at the starting line. Finally, she touched her husband's shoulder and quietly spoke into his ear. Then, leaving his side, she came over to us and simply said, "Let him try. He'll come back. I promise. Trust me. He'll come back." Jim and I looked at each other with a mix of worry and hope. After a moment's hesitation, we agreed to give Hogan a chance. India and Georgia were handed off to other campers who were willing to help and enthused to see just what Hogan would do. Jim then jogged his way to the far end of the field while I carefully listened to Trina's directions. As she prepared me on how to handle the pup during his release and finish, the crowd of campers on the knoll to the right of the field grew larger. The knowledge of Hogan's deafness had spread across camp throughout the week, and many campers were astounded at his ability to learn, perform, and succeed. They also witnessed the unyielding bond and devotion between Hogan and me. Silence replaced the roar of their usual cheering, and many held their hands over their mouths in great anticipation.

Tom asked, "Are you ready, Connie?"

"I don't know about me, but I know Hogan's ready to go," I answered as I unhooked his leash and held onto his collar with a white-knuckle grip.

"When the bunny comes around the wheel to the first pulley, let him go," Tom repeated Trina's earlier instructions. "Get ready."

As soon as the motor started and the bunny came whipping around that big wheel and the first pulley, I released my grasp. Hogan was free. He ran faster than he ever had, and he was determined to catch the prize. What unrestrained freedom! The profound silence of the group remained unbroken. I had tears streaming down my cheeks. Jim had to wipe his face with his sleeve. There literally wasn't a dry eye to be found. Hogan dashed at each corner and rushed across every stretch. He ran the entire course staying sharply focused every inch of the way. As he rounded the last bend and entered the final lap, I positioned myself to pick him up when the bunny came to a stop.

Trina called out over the sound of the motor, "Let him catch it so he feels successful! He has to win."

Hogan was elated to capture his prey which he shook ferociously. The crowd's silence broke into a jubilant uproar of applauding and hollering. Hogan had

shredded the plastic bag by the time I signed for him to "drop." The swarm of campers was stunned that he dropped his trophy. He unbelievably obeyed and dropped the bunny. Well, almost obediently. He couldn't resist one last try to get it as I grappled to lead him away. Hogan came back. He came back just like Trina promised, having had the absolute best time of his life running free.

I knew that his heart pounded, and he panted with his tongue hanging as far out as it possibly could. The muscles in his entire body had gone flat out, and every drop of his energy was drained. There was no better feeling. Hogan got to go again after a rest, and he ran with just as much thrill of the chase. He was on top of the world.

Georgia ran the course with success, but India took one look at it and walked in the opposite direction. It seemed as if she was thinking, "I'm not going to chase a plastic bag. Where's my Frisbee?" She strolled directly out to the middle of the field and did her "business." Needless to say, I was mortified. Jim was entertained by India's antics while Trina laughed so hard that her sides hurt. She declared, "Well, I guess India just told us what she thinks about lure coursing!"

It was the last day of camp and activities shifted into showcasing all the pups' accomplishments and new talents. Some of them took the form of fun competition, and almost everyone won at something. The beginner's agility classes competed against each other to see who could run the obstacles with the greatest accuracy and fastest time. Teams were made up of two dogs with their humans, so India and Hogan joined together to make a team. "On your mark, get set, go," and India took off with Jim

signaling her which direction to run and which piece of equipment to conquer.

As soon as she ripped across the line, Hogan and I shot out. He couldn't have had a better performance as he streaked back across the finish line. We won! We had the best time and cleanest run. Everyone shouted and scurried over with hugs and praise. Once again, I had tears streaming down my face as I cried, "He can do anything. He's 'normal.' Hogan can do anything."

The week couldn't have ended on a better note, and Hogan was in for yet another wonderful surprise. Secretly, Jim approached Tom and Trina to inquire what he would need to create a lure course at home. This wonderful couple beamed knowing the clandestine plan as they provided Jim with all the information and paperwork to order the equipment. Tom graciously offered to build us our very own lure course package complete with the motor, wheel, pulleys, and string. All we needed to obtain by ourselves were the "bunnies." Hogan was going to have his very own lure course to run whenever Jim could set it up.

Camp ended, and we were single-minded in our decision to sign up for camp the following year. As we began to share our goodbyes with our new, wonderful friends, a lovely young woman walked across the field to gather her belongings. Jim asked her, "Hi, do you recognize me?" She studied his face and twisted her eyebrows without recollection.

"You were a student in my physics class at Daniel Hand High School," Jim hinted.

"Oh, my goodness. You're Mr. Bombaci. What a surprise! It's been a few years," she said.

"I wasn't sure if you'd remember me or not, but I knew it had to be you, Michelle."

The two of them continued to talk as I threw the Frisbee a few last times for India and lunged Hogan and Georgia on the long lines. I wanted to make sure that they were ready to sleep on the long ride home. During their chat, Jim discovered that Michelle had attended veterinary school and recently married. He let her know he was getting our dogs a lure course, and she and her pup were invited to join us anytime. Luring was a frenetic activity, and the stimulation of more dogs always created a more exhilarating mindset. Furthermore, this fateful reunion and luring venture were going to pave the way for a future success that none of us saw coming.

We continued to attend camp for many years. When Tom's schedule prevented him from attending the June session, Jim got to run the lure course. Trina called Hogan a legend and dubbed the lure field Hogan's Heath, complete with its very own sign.

Each year Hogan learned more and participated in a wider assortment of activities. He passed the Canine Good Citizen (CGC) test and achieved Therapy Dog (TD) certification. India and Georgia followed suit. I was asked to lecture on the experiences of living with deaf dogs, showcase some of our television appearances, and demonstrate the technique of ASL with deaf and hearing pups.

*Hogan's hope was for everyone to realize anything is possible if you don't give up believing.*

*If you believe, you will receive whatever you ask for in prayer.*
Matthew 21:22 NIV

*Once you choose HOPE, anything is possible.*
Christopher Reeve

# A Rising Star

Hogan's prominence grew as he encountered and impressed more people. As a result, talk spread and folks made referrals to various media organizations. The publicity increased the requests for news coverage and features spotlighting his ability to live a normal life.

*Good Morning America* emphasized his aptitude in a segment called "Animal Intelligence." The producers highlighted his understanding of ASL, his following my instructions, and his cleverness in figuring out how to solve different problems that they presented to him. The crew watched with intrigue as Hogan found the ball in the three-cup shuffle, opened a container to get to its contents of goodies, and uncovered a hidden object.

Disney invited us to attend their gala in New York City's Central Park (1996) called "World's Largest Dog Party," where we were privileged to meet Jane, one of the people I had been helping for several years via the Internet. She was passionate about working with her two rescued, deaf Dalmatians named Dotty and Spotty. They were delightful and together we enjoyed each other's company while strolling along the path which edged the park's perimeter. When a storm suddenly came at the tail end of our jaunt, three dripping-wet humans and five drenched dogs piled into Jim's van. The pups shook until the inside of the vehicle appeared as wet as outside. Pups perched themselves in the back seats while Jane sat in the middle of the puddled floor. If laughter could raise the roof, the top of the van would have been blown away. And, of course, because the pups were behaving so well while being crammed together, cookies were dished out.

It was Jane who first stated, "He's so regal, Connie, absolutely regal. I am just amazed at how confident he looks sitting up with such perfect, confident posture. You'd never know that he came from a life of horrific abuse."

I am sure that Hogan felt regal but humble. His confidence had been cultivated by his family and all the undertakings that we accomplished together thus far. He wouldn't have his assurance if he hadn't been rescued, and he wouldn't have survived if I hadn't been given the opportunity to save him. His rehabilitation was possible because someone gave credence to his worth. Bottom line, he was resplendent because someone confirmed that he was worthy.

Disney World later contacted me hoping that we would fly to Florida to appear in one of their shows. However, the filming was scheduled only a day away, and it was mid-summer. I regretfully declined their invitation because of transportation. Flying in the heat was definitely out of the question because I believed Hogan's safety was paramount.

Soon after the events, *Dateline* producer, Betsy Osha telephoned our home and knocked on our front door within the week to scope out a possible story. She received a tip from Jane about Hogan, the deaf dog who could understand sign language, and wanted to develop a story entitled, "Deaf Sentence." Betsy and Hogan formed an instant friendship, and sensing that she was a dog lover meant that the pups liked her in the same manner. She marveled at Hogan's understanding of ASL and his response to me when talking to him. Of course, Georgia entertained her while they sat next to each other on the sofa in the barn room. Georgia was relentless in her demands for affection, and Betsy laughed as she gave in to Georgia's insistent nudging of her arm for some good pampering.

"He's so wonderful, Connie. And he's such a handsome fella," Ms. Osha stated. She asked an array of questions and probed every aspect of life with a deaf dog. After returning to her office in New York City and presenting the concept to her management, production date was set. She determined that Hogan's life was a story worth telling and wanted to cover as many chapters of his life as possible. To enhance the segment, Ms. Osha wanted to include footage of our interactions with children when I took the pups for visits to schools and churches. She also wondered if there might be a deaf student in one of the classes who would be able to communicate with Hogan and Georgia.

I contacted the superintendent of the school system where I worked as Associate Principal, and he responded with instantaneous endorsement about the prospect of "getting the word out." After his recommendation as to which of the three elementary schools in the district to contact, Principal Fitzpatrick responded, "This would be an honor, Connie. What do you need? What can we do to help?"

"We're going to need to make sure that there are no students in the class who are allergic to dogs," I said. "Also, is it possible to find out whether any of the students are afraid of dogs? Maybe they can go to the library or sit towards the back of the room where they can merely watch."

"Sure. I can take care of those things. Anything else?" asked the principal.

I inquired, "Are there any hearing-challenged students enrolled at the present time?"

"As a matter of fact, we do have a student. His name is Joey, and he's a darling boy. He goes out to a different school for classes, but I'll get in touch with his grandmother right away. I'll ask if it's okay for him to stay here that day and be involved. I think that our parents' organization would truly enjoy helping out in any way possible. How about we have some refreshments ready for the *Dateline* crew when they come?" Principal Fitzpatrick couldn't be more accommodating.

Dennis Murphy was the on-air correspondent and arrived at our home with Ms. Osha along with a complete film crew. For the next 36 hours, they filmed, interviewed, followed, and participated in every facet of living with Hogan, his canine sisters, and human parents.

It was another extraordinary time of high spirits, and mutual admiration shared among the group. I could only guess that the crew must have been expressly selected for this story because of their unmistakable appreciation of the pups and their incessant desire to give them attention. Between shoots, they chased balls, gobbled treats, and reveled in their gentle touches.

The first day was spent in our home shooting a large part of the documentary footage and material. Lights were set up, scenes created, and cameras rolled. Mr.

Murphy and the crew put all of us at ease, and there was an authentic sense of camaraderie. Everything went remarkably well, and nothing about our lives went

undisclosed. Segments even incorporated bedtime which depicted the entertaining scenario of Jim struggling for his spot in bed. The crew lost their composure when demure, little Miss Georgia was the holdout who stole his place. She wouldn't give it up without being physically lifted and moved over. Jim won, as it always should be.

Day two started at the break of daylight. I hadn't gotten my coffee when the crew came knocking on the door. The kitchen became a lively hub of activity and the first scene of the day. Cameras were placed on the floor while the pups were instructed to sit, stay, and wait for permission to eat their breakfast. Only after the pups were fed did the people get their much-needed coffee.

Next, the dogs loaded into my Jeep to wend our way to the elementary school. It looked like a convoy with the entire *Dateline* crew and their vehicles trailing behind. The class of children scheduled for the day's visit was anxiously awaiting our arrival as they prepared their lessons of ASL. As we made our entrance at the front of the classroom, they were sitting on the floor in a semi-circle. Their little faces showed excitement, and their eyes smiled. The teacher greeted us and stood next to us while members of the parents' group viewed from the back of the room behind the children. They, too, nearly burst with anticipation as several stood to see their children communicate with deaf pups.

The purpose of our visit was to allow the children to use their newly acquired knowledge of sign language with Hogan and Georgia. To get things started, I held onto their tethers until everyone heard the guidelines of good behavior, the proper ways to get the dog's attention and offer treats, as well as other basics that would govern their interaction. To further enhance the experience and simulate what the pups and Joey experience every day, I instructed students and adults to remain completely silent. Only I could speak. The bottom line was that all of us would be quiet, slow with signs and gestures, and gentle in our touches.

Joey's identity hadn't been disclosed to either the *Dateline* crew or me; and because everyone remained silent and used only ASL to communicate, it wasn't obvious who he was at first glance This anonymity served to amplify the quality of this magical experience. At least for a little while, everyone was "equal" in the method of getting their messages across, and there was a huge appreciation of just how important clear communication is in establishing a rapport.

As the children started talking with Hogan and Georgia and as the pups responded to their loving gestures, the adults, including the *Dateline* crew, wept tears of joy. The cameraman bent his head to wipe his eyes on his sleeve, and the sound person tried to hide her emotions and used the corner of her jacket to dry her face. In due course, Joey was introduced. The sight of his unadulterated glee made emotions soar, and the box of tissues from the teacher's desk was emptied as it circulated throughout the room.

"I would never have believed it if I hadn't seen it with my own eyes," stated one parent.

Principal Fitzpatrick gratefully professed, "Thank you so much for allowing us to host your wonderful visit. We all have learned an enormously important lesson, and we are all the better because of it. I honestly believe that this will be a lasting memory for our students. I know that I will always remember this day."

I asked Joey if he would like to hold onto one of the pups for a while as he walked around school. He signed a resounding, "Yes!" Together they had a

fantastic time roaming the hallways, stopping to see the secretaries in the main office, and going to visit the staff in the library. Hogan did everything that Joey told him to do. Hogan loved people, especially children.

The *Dateline* coverage brought great attention to the plight of deaf dogs. Over a thousand emails came in with the overwhelming majority expressing positive support and new understanding. People were learning fast that deaf dogs can learn and can live active quality lives. Deafness does not have to doom a pup to certain destruction any more than deafness does for humans. Humans can easily make accommodations. Understanding, acceptance, and love make a world of difference and transform attitudes. The word was out, and it caused people to think and change their beliefs.

The hope and encouragement garnered during those hours with the elementary school class created an enduring memory. Principal Fitzpatrick was correct. When Joey advanced through the grades and entered the school where I worked, we spent many times together over the four years of his high school career. We walked the halls, and Hogan ran across the fields where Joey played on the varsity football team. I think you could say that Joey was like Hogan. People communicated with and adapted for him so he could understand and play sports. Folks communicated with and adapted for Hogan so he could understand and play canine sports. Hogan and Georgia waited for him after several of his varsity games, and he always went to one knee, took off his helmet, and signed to the pups. His loyalty was steadfast, and the pups deemed him as a forever friend.

Hogan and I were stunned with the amount of interest in our story. We received many requests from various media sources and based our decisions to participate on their bona fide desire to report the real facts and to help deaf dogs. Hogan's message was important, and it had to be articulated with accuracy and compassion.

Hogan appeared in two different segments on the television series, *Amazing Tails,* on The Animal Planet network. The first piece highlighted Camp Gone to the Dogs and focused on Hogan's ability to assimilate into the camp's programs just like any other pup despite his inability to hear.

*Dateline* also produced a second story entitled, "Analyze This," which showcased Dr. Dodman and his extraordinary work assisting Hogan in conquering his compulsive behavior of pacing-pawing. He referred to Hogan as a Velcro dog who was undeniably glued to me but who was exceptionally intelligent as well. He *was* intelligent, and he took great pleasure visiting with Dr. Dodman. He appeared to feel the doctor's belief in his worth which prompted his outstanding response to his intervention. Dr. Dodman shared our beliefs and constantly conveyed kindness. In Hogan's life, respect begot respect and love created love.

Local Connecticut television stations also produced news segments. The local ABC affiliate twice featured stories about Hogan and Georgia. The first was in their "Positively Connecticut" feature with Diane Smith, and the second was years later in a reproduction of our important story, "Living with Deaf Dogs," with Jocelyn Maminta. The producer and talent, Diane Smith, from "Positively Connecticut," also reproduced her feature with us for Connecticut Public Television (CPTV). Furthermore, she included us in her book, *Absolutely Positively Connecticut*, which was a compendium of her favorite stories collected statewide over the years.

I was proud when my television students produced and received award recognition by the local FOX network and the national CNN student news programs for their stories on the pups' deafness, their ability to understand ASL, and their capacity to lead normal lives.

*Reading Rainbow* asked Hogan to sit next to LaVar Burton high atop a fire engine during an episode paying tribute to the unsung heroes from the terrorist attack in New York City on September 11, 2001. I was quiet and respectful, and Hogan sensed the serious atmosphere in this situation. With help from these men of immeasurable valor, Hogan was lifted to his perch on the edge of the truck's highest platform next to this famed personality. As Mr. Burton introduced each segment that highlighted the one-year anniversary of 9/11, we felt proud to honor our heroes.

However, even during the most solemn of occasions, a touch of humor can be welcome. I was crouched just beneath the lens of the television camera so Hogan would see me signing directions on what to do. Mr. Burton, who had been flawless during his performance, became so intrigued by our interaction that he lost his place in his lines. The firemen grinned and laughed, "Leave it to a pup, a deaf one at that, to listen better than we do!" Hogan had performed to perfection.

Hard-copy publicity also helped in spreading our message and included local newspapers, town newsletters, various organizations' newsletters and journals, pet magazines, and even *The New York Times*. All of them gave exposure to successful living with a deaf dog. Astoundingly this recognition spread internationally. I spoke on the live, Japanese radio talk shows, "Zip Morning Buzz," and "Tokyo Today." The list went on and on and on. Hogan and I didn't care about name recognition or popularity. We cared that deaf dogs were treated well, respected, and loved.

*Hogan's hope was that deafness no longer meant*
*a death sentence for deaf dogs.*

*But the eyes of the Lord are on those who fear Him,*
*on those whose hope is in His unfailing love,*
*to deliver them from death and keep them alive in famine.*
Psalm 33:18-19 NIV

# Favorite Things

*Clap your hands, all you nations;*
*Shout to God with cries of joy*
Psalm 47:1 NIV

Truth be told, each day was better than the one before. Our lives were flooded with wonderful recollections that ranged from the mundane to the extraordinary. However, each one lent special importance to Hogan's growth and created experiences that offered triumphs for the deaf pup. Each day was a gift, a new adventure. Every day was a moment held closer

to my family's hearts. Hogan thrived in peace, joy, and love. As he began to realize that his hope for a good life was a reality and experienced all kinds of wonderful phenomenon, he definitely had some special things that he liked most of all.

*A joyful heart makes the face cheerful*
Proverbs 15:13a NIV

\* \* \*

## Mischief

Hogan and his canine sisters may have been well behaved, but they also got into their fair share of mischief. Their love of play every so often led them down the path of wrongdoing. Sometimes the pups played tricks on us. These canine creatures could be crafty. Whenever Hogan could, he tried to engage me by ducking behind the sofa and drawing me into a rousing game of chase. He hovered at the corner and carefully poked his face out just far enough to catch a glimpse of me. He was sure that I didn't know that he was there and when I came close, out he bounded. Around the room, we scurried, hollered and barked, and then plunked down breathlessly next to each other on that very sofa. Hogan's reward for the gentle play was a good rubdown, and a kiss planted smack in the middle of his forehead.

Another one of his tricks was to hide the ball or rope that I was tossing in a game of fetch. After 10 or 15 minutes of this energetic exercise, Hogan took his toy and placed it out of sight behind a tree. As I searched and closed in on finding it, he charged from behind, snatching up the toy in time to run off with the prize. He pranced about with head held high, tossing the toy high in the air.

Georgia, his coy little sister, had her own mischievous behavior that brought us merriment. She was full of tricks yet masterful at portraying innocence. Her sweet face helped to create this deception. She became skilled at getting everyone else in trouble while she looked completely incapable of committing any sort of misdeed. She got all three pups involved but was seldom considered by us to be the originating culprit. In one of Georgia's dexterous pranks, Jim was even considered to be the guilty party.

Every morning, without fail, Jim and I took the pups on a long, tiring walk before heading off to work at our schools, leaving them cozy in their crates which were lined up in a row. What a shock it was to me one day when I walked in the side door and found the crates empty, their doors wide open, and India and Hogan romping around the house. Georgia, of course, was curled up in the corner of the sofa in the barn room and was sound asleep. India and Hogan darted to greet me, and Hogan went immediately into a play bow in a plea to get me to take them outside for a good sprint around the yard. I was baffled. The logical explanation had to be that the crates had not been latched properly.

When Jim arrived home later that evening, I inquired, "Did you put the pups in their crates before you left this morning?"

"Sure did," Jim replied. "Why do you ask?"

"Well, they were out of their crates, and India and Hogan greeted me at the door when I came home this afternoon. Are you sure you latched them tight?"

"I do every morning. It's the last thing I do," he insisted.

"Okay," I accepted his answer. "I just don't have a clue how they would have gotten out."

The next afternoon, once again, the pups were out of their crates and cheerfully met me at the door.

"Jim, India, and Hogan met me at the door again. Could we look at the latches and see if they're being closed? Maybe they're worn out and not staying fastened anymore."

Jim sensed that I wasn't sure that he was indeed securing them in their beds, but he dutifully complied. Together we latched and unlatched the cages. The following morning, I stayed longer than usual to help Jim put them in their pens. Yet again, when I walked into the house, India and Hogan bounded for the door in high spirits to welcome me home. In this case, three times was not in any way, shape, or form a charm for me. I was stumped. Subsequently, to get to the bottom of the mystery, we set up a video camera in the room to record the pups' activity. No more than 30 minutes after we headed out to work, Georgia also went to work. First, she used her paw to carefully hit the crate's door lever to make it go from pointing down toward the floor to pointing up. Two or three gentle slaps with her right paw accomplished step one of her ingenious plan. Then, with her nose, she gently nudged the latch to the right, freeing it from being locked. Presto! The door was ajar and out she went by pushing on the door with the top of her head. One, two, three—mission accomplished.

However, being a loving little sister, she shared her expertise to free India and Hogan as well. Because the crates had two levers on them, it took her a bit longer. But, before long, they were joyfully running from one room to the next. By day's end, Georgia was innocently sleeping while India and Hogan continued their escapades. With the mystery solved, Jim and I placed the escape artist in one of the crates that had two locking levers. For some unknown reason, she was only able to free herself from the inside when there was just one lock on the door.

A day or two passed with no pups greeting me at the door when I asked Jim, "What do you think of leaving the pups out of their crates during the day? Other than escaping their crates, they didn't seem to get into trouble."

"I'm okay with it. Give it a try. We can always go back to putting the pups back into their cages."

I guess I missed getting those wonderful, wholehearted greetings when I arrived home after a long day at work—pure joy!

*Hogan's hope was to pour out the joyful spirit of his heart freely.*

*As you enter the home, give it your greeting.*
Matthew 10:12 NIV

*Now the Lord is the Spirit, and where the Spirit of the Lord is, there is freedom.*
2 Corinthians 3:17 NIV

\* \* \*

*This is the day that the Lord has made. Let us rejoice and be glad in it.*
Psalm 118:24 NASB

## Mornings

Getting ready for work in the morning was perpetually packed with a full-scale hustle and bustle. Feeding and walking the pups, securing the house, dressing, and performing last-minute chores became a fast-paced dance with Jim and me waltzing about in an ideal partnership. We completed every task because of our perfectly-timed and harmonious choreography.

The morning's to-do list included me letting the pups outside immediately following their breakfast. I then called them into the house by flicking the backdoor light on and off. On one particular, cold, dark morning, in came Georgia with India right on her heels. Hogan wasn't with them. Without much concern, I grabbed my flashlight and proceeded out into the yard to call Hogan from his explorations of nighttime visitors. Exploring was another one of his favorite things. However, he was not in the yard. My uneasiness began to rise as I wrapped my robe more tightly around my waist to better resist the frigid air, and I jogged around the perimeter of the house. Hogan was nowhere to be found.

I rushed into the house and yelled up the stairs, "Jim, I can't find Hogan! He isn't in the yard! I'm going down the street. I need you fast! Hurry! Please, hurry!" I knew that every second counted.

Jim jumped dripping from the shower, quickly grabbed his clothes, and dressed. By now, I was running as fast as I could in my robe and slippers down the dark street. My thoughts shifted all over the place. "Where could he be? I checked the batteries in his collar just yesterday."

Flashing the light back and forth from one side of the street to the other and into the woods revealed no signs of him. I was hoping that the whiteness in his coat would reflect the light and help me find him. The more steps I took, the more frenzied I became with worry. With every passing moment, I feared that he would get too far away from home to know his way back.

By the time Jim had his keys to begin his search by car, I had run completely around the block.

"I can't find him," I cried.

"I'll go by car and see if I can find him. Maybe he'll be just down the road. He couldn't have gotten far, Connie," Jim tried to reassure me. "We'll find him."

Breathless, I ran inside and up the staircase to change into warmer clothing. My teeth were chattering as I shivered from the cold and panic of Hogan's disappearance. As I sat down on the bed to pull on my socks, my hip butted up against something hard beneath the bed covers. I tossed down the blanket and to my disbelief, there was Hogan. He was "snug as a bug in a rug," and he was awakened when I scooped him up into my arms, giving him the biggest bear hug ever. He was warm, cozy, and sleepy-eyed and seemed puzzled about all the fuss.

Hogan must have slipped back into the house when I turned away from the door to get the flashlight. Heart-pounding exhaustion jumbled with my relief, but as the adage says, "All's well that ends well."

*Hogan's hope was that life be filled with endless happiness in the midst of his forever family.*

*'Rejoice with me; for I have found my sheep which was lost!'*
Luke 15:6 NASB

\* \* \*

## Auntie 'Nette

No matter what day of the week it was, Hogan absolutely loved going everywhere with other members of our family and me. He adored being around people, and it didn't matter where or when.

One of these opportunities included the adventure of packing into the van and traveling to Delaware to visit with my sister, Annette, AKA Auntie 'Nette. She always had plenty of cookies and yummy treats in an enormous Mason jar on the corner of her kitchen counter for the pups. Not only did she have these savories, but she was like a big kid who played tug of war with Hogan as if it was her favorite game of all time. She never tired of being with the pups and unfailingly dropped treats from the cutting board as she prepared dinner. One, two, or three of the pups lined up like good children, synchronized tails wagging back and forth, waiting patiently for any tidbit that might fall to the floor. She knew exactly where to drop the scraps so all three could take their well-behaved turn in seizing the offerings.

Auntie 'Nette was proud of her furry relatives. She loved to show them off to her friends and decided to introduce them to her minister and his daughter, Bethany, who was deaf. Hogan appeared ecstatic when Bethany came skipping out of her home and instantly began talking to him in ASL. Like the young woman at the Pet Expo, her family thought that they would never be able to have a dog who understood their daughter. Hogan was the sunshine on that cloudy day. Another mutual bond formed, and for several years before she went off to the university, Bethany and Hogan often spent time together when we went to see Auntie 'Nette.

Hogan even got to help with the Sunday school class that Auntie 'Nette taught, and he interacted with the youngsters who were studying God's unconditional love and *hope*. When we visited groups of children, we all learned great lessons on acceptance and true caring. It didn't matter what size, shape, or color we were, and it didn't matter what gifts or talents we had. What did matter was that each one of us could certainly demonstrate love and respect for God's living creations and become more like the family He intends us to be.

*Hogan's hope was that children learn to*
*love and care for all God's creatures.*

*Just ask the animals, and they will teach you.*
*In His hand is the life of every creature and the breath of all mankind.*
Job 12:7, 10 NIV

\*   \*   \*

## Sunday School

Back at home, my own Sunday school classes provided unique entertainment for Hogan, Georgia, and the students. The children's eyes sparkled when the pups entered their worship hall, and Hogan became animated just waiting for them to pet and play with him. Because the children were so smitten with the pups, the teacher decided to involve them in the weekly lessons and Bible story skits. There were wonderful lessons to be learned, and the four-legged additions created the perfect atmosphere to reinforce the messages. Who would have ever thought that two deaf dogs' good behavior and example could earn them a regular spot in the membership of the class?

Celebrating the sacred meaning of Christmas was paramount, and the pups brought unique entertainment with their special appearance in the children's Christmas pageant. Hogan and Georgia were dressed up with wings and halos and dubbed the Arf Angels. The children giggled as the dogs practiced their designated roles. These amusing Arf Angels focused intently on performing their parts to perfection. Hogan listened and obeyed the silent cues 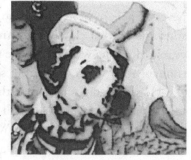 without a glitch which resulted in everyone learning and responding in harmony. Youngsters who were once reluctant to come to church started looking forward to attending and went gung-ho into learning their lines for the presentation in front of the entire congregation. Hogan made a difference. A deaf dog who was once thought to be a worthless and dumb animal had inspired children to want to learn and to love.

*Hogan's hope was that everyone believes that they are special, worthy, and smart.*

> *I pray that your life will be strong in love and built on love.*
> Ephesians 3:17b ERV

\* \* \*

## Christmas

Christmas in our family is a season overflowing with joy, celebration, and love. The pups quickly learned the sign for Christmas with their stockings (or should I say, "sacks?") making it clear because of the piles of yummy goodies

hidden inside. I sewed each of them a huge, red velvet stocking in the shape of Santa's sack and embroidered their names on the white satin cuff. When these "stockings" came out to be hung on the mantle, Hogan leapt with anticipation and barked at the prospect of getting treats all wrapped up in white tissue paper. I had to be careful, however, because Hogan thought that any tissue-wrapped gift was a puppy gift, a lesson I learned quite by accident. Without giving it a second thought, I wrapped a present for a friend in tissue paper and placed it beneath our Christmas tree. When

I returned an hour later, tissue paper covered the barn-room floor from one side to the other. Hogan must have believed that it was fair game since it was wrapped in "puppy" paper. I had to admit that he was very thoughtful. He cleverly unwrapped it without any damage to the beautiful candle inside. In fact, it was standing upright in the middle of the room shimmering in the afternoon sunlight that streamed through the vaulted windows. Gift safe. Lesson learned.

*Hogan's hope was that everyone experiences the true gifts of Christmas—peace-filled joy, abundant blessings, and unconditional love.*

*Oh come, let us sing to the Lord!*
*Let us shout joyfully to the Rock of our salvation!*
Psalm 95:1 NKJV

*May the God of hope fill you with joy and peace as you trust in Him,*
*So that you may overflow with hope by the power of the Holy Spirit.*
Romans 15:13 NIV

\*   \*   \*

## Applause

Hogan loved applause for his accomplishments. Whether he visited schools where children studied how to take good care of their pets, Sunday school classes where youngsters learned that God loves every one of His creatures, or university ASL courses in which students learned how signing could be used with animals, he became tenacious in his determination to do his best. Seeing people clapping for him provided encouragement and his confidence soared. Their enthusiasm was contagious and intensified his energy. He tried harder at whatever he was doing and wanted the clapping and smiles to prevail. He loved the attention and accolades for his behavior and achievements. Even coming when called was so much more fun as he charged towards me awaiting his arrival with applause and approval.

*Hogan's hope was to always "hear" the roar of approval.*

> *You will go out in joy and be led forth in peace;*
> *the mountains and hills will burst into song before you,*
> *and all the trees of the field will clap their hands.*
> Isaiah 55:12 NIV

\*     \*     \*

## New Home

Hogan was passionate about lure coursing, and Jim surprised us all by ordering our very own system to use whenever we wanted. There was just one problem—we didn't have a yard large enough to map out the course and set up the equipment. However, when Jim decides to set his mind to something, especially for the ones he holds dear, nothing gets in the way of him executing the task. Jim's love is selfless, and several times a week he loaded the weighty equipment into the back of his van and drove the pups to a public park. He went about setting up the course for the pups' amusement. By inviting other dogs to lure with them, the sport became immensely more fun and energizing. And, as Jim promised his former student, Michelle, at camp, he frequently extended an invitation to her and her pup, Jazz.

Often passersby lined the perimeter of the field to watch as the dogs coursed at top speed, darting around curves and corners while chasing the bunny. Their amazed faces watched as the pups participated in a novel, high-velocity competition. I wondered who was more entertained—the dogs or the humans watching the dogs.

Michelle regularly joined us and on one occasion asked, "Would you mind if I invited a friend and her dog to come along with me? I think she'd love this. In fact, I am certain of it. She's a fellow veterinarian, and I highly respect her. I know that we wouldn't have to worry about her or her pup. She'd be very responsible in controlling her dog."

Without hesitating, Jim agreed, "Sure. It would be even more exciting for the dogs and would certainly put our equipment to more use." He jokingly added, "Besides, it'll add more people who can help set out and pull up the pulleys."

He knew full well that her recommendation would be a person and a pup who could be trusted to be well behaved and suited for the game. The very next time we went to the field to lure, Michelle was already there, waiting to help us set up.

Her friend was with her, and I was especially overjoyed because I immediately recognized that she was Doctor Ouellette's assistant, Dr. Lynda Perry. Who would have thought? Dr. Perry took care of the pups several times and always provided them with the kind of love and caring that every pup and owner desires. It's a small world.

The pups ran at their usual top speed to show Lynda's pup just what "running the bunny" was all about. In a flash, her pup took off and returned with hanging tongue and quivering muscles. This was evidence of great joy. Lynda's eyes filled with tears realizing that her pup had experienced the time of his life, and she squatted on the field's dusty surface embracing him.

Michelle and I glanced at each other and silently decided to allow Lynda to enjoy the moment. Together we set off to pull up the pulleys and string, leaving her to enjoy that precious moment. Jim stayed behind to pack the motor, pull wheel, and other items into the storage boxes and engaged in conversation with our astonished rookie.

"The dogs sure do enjoy this silly chase," Jim acknowledged.

Lynda responded, "They sure do. May I come again?"

"Of course, anytime. I only wish that we could have this set up in our own yard, so it wasn't such a hassle to find an open field, set up the gear, and then tear it all down again for next time. It limits how much we can use it. Connie and I are keeping our eyes open for the right plot of land to build our home and have plenty of space to set the course up more permanently," Jim informed her.

"Really? A sign just went up on a beautiful plot of land on the road where I live. You've got to go take a look."

"Wow, I have to tell Connie. I know she's going to want to see it," he replied.

She added, "I live just a couple miles away, and it's on a very quiet, dirt road."

When Jim and Lynda told me about the property, I could scarcely contain my zeal. "Let's go!"

"Okay, let's swing by on our way home and take a look," Jim agreed. He could never resist my requests.

The lot wasn't more than five miles from our current home. A 500-foot driveway led to the parcel that was situated behind a front property with a small, weather-beaten, historic home. The pups were pooped and content to sleep in the van while we walked through the pine forest on the mushy driveway. We jumped puddles, straddled fallen trees, and sank ankle-deep in mud before we reached the end of the lengthy path which opened to a large open field. Brush and small trees covered the area because of years of neglect, but we were awe inspired. Its beauty was incredible, and we envisioned our dream home.

"Oh, Jim. This is perfect," I spoke in a hushed voice. "Do you think it's big enough? Do you think you can build on it? Do you think our home will be suitable for this lot? Do you...."

"Connie, let's take a breath and walk farther down the lot. We need to take a good look," Jim tried to calm my excitement. He didn't want me to be disappointed but he, too, shared the same level of excitement.

Upon returning to the van, we saw the pups were still sound asleep recuperating from their strenuous play. I searched for my cell phone and looked at Jim stating, "Honey, let's call the number on the sign."

Twenty minutes later, the seller arrived. More walking and lots of talking took place, and we processed all the information. Soon after he left, I said, "Let's call him again and tell him that we want to put down a deposit, Jim. We don't want to lose it."

"I don't think that we need to rush, Connie," Jim reasoned.

I pushed, "Please. It can't hurt to put down a deposit and then explore all the tests and things that we need."

Jim hesitated. "You're really sure about this, aren't you? And you're not going to let me go home without putting down a deposit."

My face lit up as I flew across the console to smother Jim with kisses. Early the next morning the seller received multiple calls wanting to purchase the property. Several offered more than the asking price trying to land the deal, but we were first. We had put down a deposit, and the land was ours. We were going to have a new home where we could run the bunny for our pups. Because of Hogan's love of luring, I always said, "Hogan found the place for our new home which we named the Three Dog Inn."

Jim designed and built us a sensationally puppy-friendly, post-and-beam home which was complete with dog doors, barn wood floors, underground fence, doggie pond, outside bathing table, and a huge, front yard for our lure course. When the massive logs were delivered to the scene of our future home, Jim systematically notched and numbered each one to ready them for an old-fashioned, barn raising. More than thirty friends and family members generously offered to wield a hammer and muster their muscles to join the building party. We all gathered on a cloudless Saturday morning in mid-June. Armed with spikes, sledgehammers, ladders, diagrams, and a plethora of other apparatus, workers took their assigned positions. The teamwork hummed like a well-oiled machine. Posts were carried on site, hoisted into place, and secured with precision by each of the builders.

The pups hung out with a handful of women and me in the camper that we converted into the chuck wagon. Pots and pans bubbled with delicious food to nourish the work crew throughout the day, and jugs of ice water lined the perimeter of the job site. Some people weren't able to lend a hand in the actual erection of the house's frame, but they were able to entertain our lively pups with strolls down our long, dirt driveway. While the walks were an amusing distraction for the dogs, the ultimate treat was being allowed to lick clean the bottoms of the empty cookware when the last helpings were scooped out by the famished humans. Of course, I monitored which food pans were puppy-safe.

The summer sun beat down on the workers' backs, and sweat soaked their clothing. To help cool themselves, many of our crew wrung the sweat from their shirts over the tops of their heads and then wrapped the garments around their foreheads. They remained determined to build and erected our home one post at a time, like Lincoln Logs. As the skyline to the west turned red with the setting sun, its majestic frame stood proudly in place.

Jim labored nine months to finish our home. "Like having a baby," I joked. During this time, we lived with Romanie, a woman of extraordinary character, who worked with me in the school system. She was the kind of person who endeared herself to whomever she met and easily gave her talents, time, and energy to benefit others. Our former home quickly sold, and we literally had nowhere to sleep. There aren't many landlords who wanted to lease for an indefinite period of time or to a family with multiple pets. Learning of our plight, Romanie graciously rented us two adjoining bedrooms in her antique farmhouse set on a hill overlooking an acre pond. We were blessed with her charitable offer, and we made many splendid, mostly comical, memories with this superb, native Dutch woman. Without fail, every day was punctuated with at least one notable event or recollection. Mostly, these occasions included me trying to contain three high-spirited pups in our limited living quarters. Even though the cages took up every inch of remaining floor space in the bedrooms, the pups still managed to dart after Romanie's terrified kitty while I trailed behind them by scrambling over top the crates. Outside, I often chased behind them in the knee-deep mud around the edge of the pond while Romanie leisurely swam with the Canada geese. There were countless celebrations sprinkled with laughter creating forever memories.

Our home was created by and because of many people who gave selflessly of themselves and their services. They included family, friends, friends of friends, and family of friends. It was truly unbelievable. I never knew who or what I

would encounter on any given day, but no words could ever express the awe that enveloped the endeavor. The unlimited love of others blessed our home unmeasurably.

My sister, Annette, and her husband, Ron, drove back and forth from Delaware to Connecticut so that my parents, Grandpere and Meme, could be part of the barn raising. Romanie's brother, Jacque, on holiday from the Netherlands, offered to build embellishments to add detail to the exterior siding. Romanie, whose family frowned upon a single stone being removed from her landscape, brought a distinctive marker to become part of our fireplace and serve as a permanent keepsake of our cherished time together. My parents also surprised us and presented a brick from their home that Grandpere had built, and it projects out just above the mantle, endowing us with a memento of their unshakable love, devotion, and support.

Moving day finally arrived, and we stepped into our new homestead and a magnificent dream come true. There was only one big problem. The lure course equipment was nowhere to be found. It simply vanished into thin air. With all the volunteers who came to lend a helping hand, the container with the lure course equipment must have gotten tossed into the dumpster by accident. Our front yard's purpose was gone until Tom made and shipped us a new one. Soon the course was back up and running, and friends came to join in the frenetic sport. Hogan sprang up and down like a pogo stick impatiently waiting his turn and feverishly barking as I watched each pup race around the circuit. Indeed, we were home.

I would be remiss if I didn't mention that we had a cat named Puttee. Her name was Native American for the type of moccasins with the long, leather laces that wrap around the lower leg. I always said, "Puttee wrapped herself right around our hearts."
Our daughters, NancyLee and Heather, rescued her tiny, tortured body from the parking lot at a shopping plaza about 16 years before. Puttee fancied our new home constructed of rugged timbers spanning across the open-space design as her playhouse. She could easily escape the three pups by lying on the overhead rafters as if they were the limbs of her personal tree. She taunted the pups as she peered down with the tip of her tail slowly swaying back and forth. I imagined her purring, "Ha. Ha. You can't get me."

Connie Bombaci

*Hogan's hope was to delight in having a comforting home where he could love his entire family and run free, untethered across that gigantic field.*

> *This hope is like an anchor for us.*
> *It is strong and sure and keeps us safe.*
> Hebrews 6:19 ERV

*      *      *

## Town Walks

I also walked the pups on Main Street's sidewalks or through flea markets on the town common to foster their well-behaved socialization. It was a perfect opportunity to meet and greet all sorts of folks and become accustomed to a variety of environments. I answered questions about living with a deaf dog. Hogan provided living proof of how to work with adopted, four-legged family members in an established and ongoing training program. Pets are real and important, and daily attention is non-negotiable just as it is for any child or loved one.

I was protective and vigilant about who and how strangers approached us. Once I felt comfortable, the pups were given the "okay" sign to greet a new friend by first acquiring a good sniff of their clasped hand. People and other dogs were never allowed to rush in. Hogan was to be on his best and most polite behavior at all times when out in public. He had to put his best paw forward.

*Hogan's hope was to meet genuine and lasting friends who believed in him.*

> *My command is this:*
> *Love each other **as I have loved you.***
> John 15:12 NIV

*      *      *

## Dancing

Hogan unreservedly loved to dance and was ready to spring into a poised position in a heartbeat. Whenever I signed, "dance," he balanced onto his hind legs and offered me his front paws to sashay around the room. I cranked up the music loud enough so that Hogan could feel the pounding of the bass instruments and drums in the air against his body and on the floor in a rhythmic beat. My favorite song for him was "My Guy," and it became a regular dancing tune. We often got to spend fantastic moments dancing together.

*Hogan's hope was always to enjoy the dance of a safe, full life with his human mama.*

*You turned my wailing into dancing;*
*You removed my sackcloth and clothed me with joy.*
Psalm 30:11 NIV

\*   \*   \*

## Baskets

Even though Hogan was now spoiled in every way, he continually searched for the comfort of a cozy, warm bed. I think that this was a result of his horrible experience of being so cold during his first, frigid winter. Being swaddled felt reassuring to him.

Much to my surprise, laundry day provided him the perfect opportunity to discover a large, wicker basket filled with clothing just waiting for him. He  climbed in and snuggled under the clothing. Only his eyes and nose were visible. I was thoroughly amused, so I quickly summoned Jim to come and see our clever boy.

Climbing into the laundry basket became a routine until the day Hogan settled into freshly cleaned clothing

AFTER running outside on a rainy day. My amusement switched gears and focused on finding another solution to make my pup happy.

"We have to find a basket for Hogan," I informed Jim who agreed after witnessing a muddy mess. Hogan lay in his soft bed looking up at us. I know he was thinking, "What? I always sleep here. Is there a problem?" I went to work searching the stores and the internet for baskets that could serve as a doggie bed. Every option was investigated when at last I found a large, wicker dog bed in a Vermont store specializing in baskets. Without a moment's hesitation, it was ordered and delivered. Hogan slept on cloud nine!

*Hogan's hope was that the warmth and security of love would always surround him.*

*For where your treasure is, there your heart will be also.*
Luke 12:34 NIV

\* \* \*

## Noontime Walks

Hogan did everything, went everywhere, and spent every day with me. He was a Velcro dog, but he was a Velcro dog who successfully dealt with his separation anxiety. Everyone was proud of him, and they wanted his contentment to continue. Dr. Dodman was an ongoing resource and suggested that Jim and I mix up our morning routines as we got ready for work. That way, Hogan wouldn't catch on that we were leaving for the day and would stay calm about the possibility of being abandoned. This was a life-long fear that needed to be quelled. Sometimes we went out the door and came right back in. Other days we took him for a walk before we dressed for work. Other days we walked immediately before we drove off. Now and again, we skipped the walk completely. We tried to be clever and unpredictable. Dr. Dodman's suggestion of these arbitrary combinations worked! Additionally, upon our departure, we gave Hogan a treat, such as a hollowed ball filled with peanut butter. It not only kept him occupied for an extended time as he worked hard at polishing off every smidgen but, more importantly, it gave him something positive that he associated with being left on his own.

His two canine sisters kept him company throughout the workday. They romped throughout the house, snoozed on the sofa and master bed, or dashed out the doggie door to spot the squirrel at the bird feeder. Hogan also loved barking at the deer passing through the woods just behind the six-foot fence that Jim constructed to create a safe haven when no one was home. But the deep-seated yearning for human's contact was imprinted on his soul.

"Nothing left to chance" was the motto I used when I added extra insurance to the plan and helped my pup have a peaceful day. The name of that assurance was Linda.

Linda was our lovely, soft-spoken neighbor who lived across our dirt road. At noon, she walked from her house to ours, coming by for a visit in the hours  that I was away. After several weeks of this routine, Hogan's internal clock became set, and he went to the gate anticipating her arrival. Her gentle demeanor conveyed kindness. Being an artist by trade, she often came with the residue of a claylike substance on her hands, and Hogan appeared to love the smell. Linda and Hogan shared a common interest as they both loved to play in the dirt. We were blessed to have Linda.

*Hogan's hope was that everyone knows the importance of kindness and faithful friendship.*

*A friend loves at all times*
Proverbs 17:17 NIV

*       *       *

## Flowers

Seasons came and went, and each had its own unique feel. In autumn,  Hogan and I danced to the tune of leaves swirling to the ground. Winter's snowy days brought back bitter memories of his being left alone in an unprotected icy pen. Spring and summer delivered warm temperatures with all the pups wading in our puppy pond and lure coursing. Much to everyone's surprise, Hogan loved flowers. They were pretty, and their delicate nature fascinated him. He studied the different petals, leaves, and scents. Purple petunias were his all-time favorite, and whenever I hung a basket of them around the outside of the house, he stood high on his hind legs and stretched as far as he possibly could so he could burrow his nose deep into the pot and inhale their strongest aroma. They smelled like happiness to him.

*Hogan's hope was that his life would be infinitely happy
and filled with the sweet scents of life.*

*Perfume and incense bring joy to the heart*
Proverbs 27:9a NIV

# Therapy Work for
# Children and Seniors

*Each of you should use whatever gift you have received to serve others,*
*faithfully administering God's grace in its various forms.*
1 Peter 4:10 NIV

Weekdays were school days, and I would take Hogan to visit classrooms of young children whenever I could free up a couple of hours in my busy work schedule. He was a smash hit with a class for deaf children. To their delight, he allowed himself to be hugged, kissed, and fussed over by each child. While he was by nature, a friendly and social animal, it became clear to me that he was exceptionally at ease interacting with kids. He also became a regular in classroom reading programs as children learned to use their voices as they read their books aloud, and he lay peacefully in the middle of their circle. Sometimes he identified the neediest of little ones. No child was going to go unloved on his watch! It was life-altering therapy for them and for Hogan. I recall the reticent little boy cowering under his desk at the far corner of the room and who was coaxed out by the persistent touch of Hogan's paw on his foot and of puppy kisses on his face. The youngster later went on to become a regular presenter in front of the entire class when we visited, and Hogan sat by his side. His hand twirled the soft ears and stroked Hogan's head and neck as he enunciated the words of his assignment with greater confidence.

We devoted our Sunday mornings to serving our elderly citizens in a nursing home. Hogan had achieved therapy dog status, so he was permitted to offer his companionship to the lonely. He greeted every resident, and many of them looked forward to our Sunday visits. Making these numerous friendships created wonderful memories of our times together. When Hogan and I entered the nursing facility, we walked into an attractive foyer lined with chairs and lofty windows. Residents who were mobile could choose to visit with their guests in this cheery setting rather than the confines of their rooms. The building consisted of two wings, and walking in either direction led us to a long corridor with rooms on both sides. The nurses' stations were located halfway down directly in the middle and provided surveillance of the entire wing.

It was mandatory for us to check in and record that we were in the building. This policy was established for safety reasons in the event of an emergency. Although, most importantly, it gave me the chance to gain information regarding new residents or those who needed some extra tender-loving care. Most of the residents were restricted to the inside of the building unless accompanied by staff or a family member. However, in exceptional situations, like that of the outgoing woman who loved to garden, they could roam throughout the bordering grounds. This joyful woman had an infectious smile and positive attitude despite her bleak circumstance. She found the silver lining in everything, and nobody could rob her of it. That was precisely how she found her calling while living away from family and friends.

"I want to stop and smell the flowers," she would tell us.

When the weather was warm and the sun shone brightly, Hogan and I often arrived to find our resident gardener adorned with a wide-brimmed hat, rolling herself here and there in her wheelchair. She eyed the plants and pulled sprouting weeds from the enormous, clay flowerpots lining the cobblestone walkway into the building. Her diligent upkeep of the flowers became her mission, something to look forward to and replace the ache in her heart. Hogan's mission became watching over our gardening lady and adding laughter to her life.

The first part was easy. He only had to sit next to her as she sat in her wheelchair and reached between the petals of her pretty flowers to pluck the weeds.

She gleefully exclaimed, "This is so much more enjoyable when I have company. You know that this is a very important job because we can't let the gardens become messy. I want everything to look perfectly beautiful for my guests when they come to see me." The heartbreak was that she never had anyone come to see her. This reality made our therapy work of grave consequence.

As she puttered around the urns, Hogan decided that the skimpy piles of weeds were savory treats since at home he nibbled on grass like a goat. He liked the sweet taste and simply took it for granted that this good-natured lady was providing him with a delicious treat. He naturally had to be polite. Watching him devour her pickings, however, brought out a cackle. She laughed so hard that she squealed, "Oh, my! It's a good thing I put on extra padding. I think that I sprang a leak!"

She called her four-legged friend "Little Rascal," and he recognized her enjoyment of his company. His demeanor perked up as she stroked his face with her arthritic hands. He and his gardener shared pleasure in their time together basking in the warmth of the sunshine as Hogan became a guardian angel to many of the residents in the nursing home.

> *Love is patient, love is kind.*
> I Corinthians 13:4 NIV

\* \* \*

There are many remarkable stories about Hogan's visits to the nursing homes. Every one tells a tale of respect and love with our senior citizens who needed unwavering devotion and steadfast friendship. Each paints a striking picture of connection and companionship. There was the woman who hadn't uttered a word for almost a year until she set eyes on my pup. She immediately shouted out, "A dog! Oh, such a wonderful dog!" There was also the scrawny, 100-year-old Anthony who coaxed Hogan into his room with a boxful of dog bones bought just for our visits. Hogan's sessions were filled with amazing and touching moments. Hogan and his senior friends accepted each other for who they were in that instant. Size, shape, color, age, condition, or frailties didn't matter.

I vividly remember a Sunday when the receptionist notified me that an older gentleman had been admitted and now resided in a private room at the far end of the hallway. He was branded a grumpy old soul who cloistered himself in his room, even for meals. The staff warned me that he would be, without doubt, unreceptive to us stopping by to say, "Hello." That's all I needed to hear. Everyone deserved a bit of cheer, and I hoped that a pup would be just what the doctor ordered. Off we trotted down the long corridor making a right-hand turn into the doorway of his room. He lay in bed, still dressed in his night clothes with disheveled hair and unshaven face. He faced away from the doorway and didn't see us standing there in silence. Together, Hogan and I just watched. Peace seemed to settle upon the room. With a despondent sigh, the man closed his eyes and slowly turned his head. A tear was streaming down his right cheek as he opened his eyes and discovered us standing close by. He didn't say a word, nor did I. Hogan looked up at me for a cue on what he should do. I smiled at the gentleman and gave him a friendly nod. We quietly left the doorway and completed our rounds.

Hogan and I revisited the next Sunday right on schedule. I routinely alternated taking India, Hogan, and Georgia, but I had Hogan accompany me again so it would be him that our gentleman would see. We made our rounds to all the other rooms first, visiting and allowing folks to fuss over my pup. Everyone looked forward to our social calls. Lastly, we made our way to the gentleman's doorway. He lay in bed, still dressed in his night clothes with disheveled hair and unshaven face. Exactly like our initial visit, he didn't say a word, nor did I. Hogan sat next to me without moving a muscle. Just as we were about to leave, I gave him a smile and friendly nod. We quietly left.

This routine continued for two or three more weeks. Hogan was happy because it was he who got to go. When I checked in, the nurses informed us that our gentleman was sitting up. They were amazed at his request to sit up today but were heartened by the slightest bit of progress. My pup obediently walked next to me directly to his doorway, and we were happy to see him sitting up in bed, no tear on his cheek. Again, we stood silently with a smile.

After a few minutes, I gave him a friendly nod and added, "Have a blessed day."

The following week when we arrived at our gentleman's doorway, he was dressed and seated on the side of his bed. Hogan and I stood quietly for a moment when I asked, "May we come in for a short visit?" He nodded, "Yes." I walked toward him and signed to Hogan to "go" and greet a "friend." He went up to the senior man and put his chin next to the man's left hand that was helping him balance as he sat with his legs dangling over the side of the bed. As he lifted his trembling hand, Hogan moved closer and placed his head against the gentleman's leg on the blankets. He stroked the top of Hogan's head with a touch that was caring, yet desperate and pain-filled. His emotions poured out of his heart and into his fingers, and Hogan remained motionless until our new friend looked up at me with a tear streaming down his right cheek.

Our purpose became clearer with each visit. Every week our gentleman made more progress. He made strides to become alive again. Upon signing in, the nurse on duty apprised us, "Your gentleman is in the bathroom right now getting help. He wanted to shave this morning." What overwhelming elation we felt. I hardly contained myself, but we visited the other residents first and then proceeded to his room as our last stop. Standing respectfully in his doorway, I asked, "May we come in for a visit?"

Our gentleman replied aloud, "I'd like that."

Our time together progressed from quiet to conversations with Hogan positioned directly at his side. As he sat in his chair, he petted my special pup with increasing strength and enthusiasm. There was a distinguished quality about this man who was poised and stately. His talks with me revealed an articulate, well-educated man. I learned that he was a renowned personality who had been recognized nationally and celebrated for his achievements in the world of media. He was, however, a person whose family abandoned and warehoused him. Hogan knew exactly what this phenomenal individual felt, and it appeared that he promised never to forsake him.

My pup kept his promise, and I sensed his urgency to see the senior every week. For months it was Hogan who went to perform therapy work, and the three of us became true friends who dedicated longer stays together. Each visit proved wonderful until one unforgettable Sunday morning. The nurse from his wing met us at the entrance before we had the chance to check in.

"He's waiting for you," she voiced clenching her hands.

I was puzzled by her expression, but Hogan knew. He never pulled on his leash, but he now yanked hard at its end. I attempted to correct him by gently pulling him toward me. He wanted nothing to do with obeying my request and yanked again.

I said, "Okay, boy. Go," and dropped his lead. He took off down the long corridor and rounded the nurses' station. He continued to sprint as the nurse and I attempted to keep up. His gentleman was in bed, still dressed in his night clothes with disheveled hair and unshaven face. Exactly like our first visit. Hogan refused to let him just lie there alone. So, one paw at a time, he climbed into the bed and settled along the length of his dear friend's body. I am sure that Hogan felt the warmth of his long, thin body and nestled closer. The man's right arm lifted and rested on the pup as he turned his face to see him. Hogan gently moved upward and put his head on his friend's chest so he could gaze into his pup's deep, loving eyes. A tear streamed down his right cheek as he took a long breath, his last breath. "I waited for you, Hogan." This impressive friend passed peacefully with the loving pup by his side. He wasn't forsaken. He knew that he was loved.

The nurse who was with me sank to the chair in tears. "You made a difference, Hogan. Thank you. Thank you so much. He waited until you got here."

Most of the staff gathered in the doorway and were speechless at the image of Hogan with his gentleman. They were stunned at how he knew that his cherished friend needed him before entering the wing. No one made the slightest effort to move Hogan from his place, and he was permitted to remain with his gentleman. He had become a magnificent icon for everyone and a welcome "ray of sunshine" as he reached out from his isolated place of abandonment to share himself with others.

*Hogan's hope was for love filled with peace*
*and serenity for his gentleman.*

*Find rest, O my soul, in God alone;*
*My hope comes from Him.*
Psalm 62:5 NIV

# Part Four

# Peace

*The fruit of the Spirit is love, joy, peace, patience, kindness, goodness, faithfulness, gentleness, and self-control.*
Galatians 5:22-23a NASB

Hogan's pure and untarnished soul touched a multitude of lives, both two-legged and four-legged alike. His tremendous light of determination and courage shined, offering the gift of inspiration to try, to dream the impossible, and to accept our personal challenges with the confidence that we can succeed. He accepted his life and gave back unconditional love. Because of his assured strength and amazing spirit, many lives have changed for the better. I didn't know what life with Hogan was going to be like before I met him, and now I can't imagine a day without him, my "Mama's Boy." I believe that Hogan was given to me by God for a reason, and his legendary life of survival, growth, and love will serve to help anyone who seeks hope.

We continue to share our hearts, and he is able to observe his wonderful life full of love realized. Hogan showed me that we are all worthy to have dreams, to be loved, and to be accepted. He taught me how to hope with the promise of happy abandon, how to hold on to hope when challenges cross its path, and how to share hope with others no matter the circumstance.

As the years passed, Hogan met older age with great valor. His body faded and became weak, but his spirit remained strong and refused to give way. His love endured and continued to inspire faith in the goodness and worthiness of all God's creations.

I believe that Hogan will always be with me and that he is watching down over me. I couldn't imagine my life without him when he was here by my side, and I still cannot imagine a day without him.

I don't know what life was like for Hogan before he became a part of our family, and I don't know what his life is like now that he is gone. But, if we let it, Hogan's spirit will continue to share his message of hope. If we open our hearts, we might just understand what Hogan has been trying to tell us all along.

Perhaps it's best, for once, to let him speak for himself.

*As for me, I will always have hope . . .*
Psalm 71:14a NIV

# My Final Days

*You are my hope, O Lord God,*
*You are my trust from my youth.*
Psalm 71:5 NKJV

The years passed by in a flash and it seemed as if I, Hogan, were 18 months old just a short while ago. My senses began to fail, but my love for Mama was greater today than yesterday. I remained her Velcro dog and unfailingly was found lying on the floor with my head on her foot every morning as she readied herself for work in front of the mirror. My life was based on hope—hope in and for each day to be filled with the grace of God's unconditional, abiding love that would protect and guide me. Many would deny that I, a mere dog, could ever think or feel in such a way. But I can attest that my heart drew nearer to the Lord with every new blessing bestowed on my life with Mama.

My eyes dimmed with my increasing age, but my spirit continued to be uplifted with unspeakable peace and in undying hope. I refused to let go of my dream for real, unfathomable life. Majestic love filled the crevices of my heart, and heaven and earth seemed to collide in this unbelievable journey of mine.

My body of brawn and stately physique also began to give way to pain and

weakness. Daily walks became slower, and my beloved lure course was set out one last time for me to try and run its path.

"I think Hogan will be injured if we let him run it, Connie," Papa said.

Mama was in denial and thought aloud, "But, he loves it so much, Jim. Maybe we can run it slower for him or maybe we can just run the bunny along one side and let him catch it. Maybe…" She realized Papa was right but wanted one last chance for me to enjoy the love of the chase.

When the motor started, I tried to jog but slipped as I approached the first corner. I turned and hobbled back to Mama who was already bending down, clapping, to receive me with her usual celebratory embrace.

"Hogan," she signed. "Good boy! Mama's good boy!"

The cart that was bought to help my older sister, India, during her later years when her hind legs became too weak to walk was resurrected for me. I didn't want to use it, and Mama could tell from the look in my eyes and my unusual lack of cooperation. I didn't like it, and I didn't want it. I just stood there and made little effort to move. I knew my fate, and I accepted its vow. Hope remained constant and trustworthy.

My life began with great distress but transformed into a dream of hope come true in every aspect. Life, as I knew it on this earth with Mama, became frail and began to fade. But, in looking into my blind eyes, their devoted light told Mama that I held fast to the belief that love existed, that faith was eternal, and that hope is endless. I told her I loved her. I told her that she gave me the gifts of faith, love, and hope.

Ten days shy of my sixteenth birthday, Mama held me tenderly in her lap and cuddled me for the last time. My days of cavorting, being mischievous, playing, and romping were over. I looked into my Mama's eyes as I faded away. A tear ran down the right side of my face. My body relaxed and rested in the loving, comforting arms of my champion cheerleader.

It didn't matter how hopeless my life started. Everything that was created after my rescue was nothing less than perfection. The inspiration of hope touched hearts and restored souls. Beliefs changed and behavior was recreated. Hope now saves lives, accepts differences without prejudice but with love.

I want everyone, especially my Mama, to be forever engaged in the magnificent day-to-day dance with life—a life of being loved, a life of being believed in, and most of all, a life of undying hope.

Days were different now. As Mama sat on the steep steps leading up to the front porch, she looked out over the giant front yard where the lure course ran. Papa put it out of sight in an attempt to help ease the pain in her heart, but she visualized in her mind and heart me running freely around the imagined perimeter of the course. She saw me cunningly outwit the elusive bunny by cutting it off across its path. In her memory I was young again, smiling and carefree. Sounds of my barking echoed in her ears.

Her chest felt as if it would break open with a heart that ached with a crushing force. She missed me so terribly yet sensed me with her. A small smile lifted the edges of her mouth as she professed aloud, "Oh, Hogan. I love you. Please know that I love you. And, dear Lord, take good care of him. Let his eternal flame shine brightly in Heaven so I can see him in the stars." With a tear-soaked face, she cried out, "I really need to know that he's all right."

Mama sat there for most of the day, returning to this same spot after the evening meal. Papa joined her, sitting silently by her side. The moon was full and lit Earth's surface with a brilliant golden glow. Looking up over the tree line beyond the open field, she caught a glimpse of a star brighter than she had ever seen. No other was there, and it didn't matter whether or not it was "supposed" to be there. All that mattered was that her Hogan endured.

*My hope is that my life offers inspiration for others to overcome any challenge and that life be filled with eternal love, unconditional acceptance, and shining hope.*

*Everything is possible for one who believes.*
Mark 9:23 NIV

*We wait in hope for the Lord;*
*He is our help and our shield.*
Psalm 33:20 NIV

*May the Lord watch between you and me*
*when we are away from each other.*
Genesis 31:49 NIV

# Afterword

Hogan taught me how to live my life as a courageous journey. I determined right then that his life was going to be "A gift that keeps on giving." Our mission was to carry on the signs of God's unconditional love and to share *Hogan's Hope.*

# About the Author

Connie Bombaci, a retired educator, is resolute in her love for animals, belief in the worthiness of all God's creations, and desire to provide encouragement no matter what the challenge. Connie is an optimist and compassionate person whose Christian faith guides her to believe in the extreme goodness and immeasurable importance of every being.

Her love for animals began in early childhood and developed from her desire to be kind. She has enjoyed many adopted pets throughout her lifetime, especially ones that have needed help, rescuing domestic and wild orphaned, injured, or abandoned animals. Her longing for others to believe in the value of themselves led her to become an educator where she worked fervently to increase young peoples' self-confidence and belief in themselves, despite any difficulty. She offered hope where frustration and failure seemed inevitable. While serving as a teacher and associate principal in a Connecticut public school system, she took great pleasure working within its community, finding it especially fulfilling to encourage and support her students, coworkers, and community members.

Connie grew up in a suburban neighborhood outside of Philadelphia, Pennsylvania and now lives in rural Connecticut with her husband, Jim, and their two rescued pups in the rustic, puppy-friendly home that Jim built on their five-acre "piece of Heaven." She also is surrounded by the love of her children, grandchildren, and great-grandchildren.

This book is the Christian edition of Connie's original version titled, Hogan's Hope: A Deaf Hero's Inspirational Quest for Love and Acceptance. While Scripture was originally included in this heartfelt story, it was removed on the advice of marketing. However, Connie's intense desire to share her faith-filled belief in Hogan's success compelled her to restore the original manuscript to this edition titled, Hogan's Hope: A Deaf Dog, a Courageous Journey, and a Christian's Faith.

Hogan's life is a blessed story of expectant triumph despite the odds and shares the message that hope can be found in the kind and generous hearts of gracious and loving people.

## Connect with Connie

www.Conniebombaci.com
www.Facebook.com/ConnieBombaci
www.Twitter.com/ConnieBombaci
www.Instagram.com/conniebombaci

2018 Benjamin Franklin Award Medalist

2017 Kindle Book Promos Book First-Prize

2017 Best Books Finalist

Readers' Favorite Five-Star Recipient

Book Designer Gold for Cover Design

# Appendix 1

## Hogan's Appearances

| Date | Examples | Information | Producer |
|---|---|---|---|
| 1994 October | CT Humane Society's Pet Expo: Greeters | CT Humane Society | |
| 1994 December 15 (Broadcast Spring 1995) | *Animal Adventures*: "Special People, Special Dogs" | Jack Hanna | |
| 1995 | Bethany | Pastor's daughter, Newark, DE | |
| 1996 | *Oprah Winfrey Show:* "Fascinating Things" (Taped in May 1996, and aired August 14, 1996) | Nicholas Dodman | Harpo Studios |
| 1996 February | CNN Student News Production: "Deaf Dogs" (Award Recipient) | Students News Production | Jason Cologni HKHS, TV Production |

| | | | |
|---|---|---|---|
| 1996 April | Fox Student News: "Deaf Dogs" | Student News Production | HKHS, TV Production |
| 1996 April | WFSB Channel 3: "Deaf Dogs" | | CBS, Connecticut |
| 1996 April | Amazing Tails: Dr. Nicholas Dodman, Professor Emeritus, Animal Behaviorist Tufts University, Boston, MA | Nicholas Dodman | Animal Planet |
| 1996 April 10 | Walt Disney's "World's Largest Dog Party" | Central Park, New York | |
| 1996 December 22 | *Dateline NBC:* "Deaf Sentence" | Dennis Murphy | Betsy Osha |
| 1996-2002 | Various Dog Walk Fundraisers (Fidelco, Rescue, etc.) | | |
| 1996-2007 | Therapy Dog Service Certified Therapy Dog & Canine Good Citizen (CGC) | | |
| **1997** | "Positively Connecticut" | | Diane Smith News 8, ABC Connecticut |
| 1997 January 15 | Japanese Radio Live "Zip Morning" with Buzz | | |

| | | | |
|---|---|---|---|
| 1997 April 10 | Played roles of Pongo & Perdy at Sophia's Birthday Party, daughter of NY Hotel Mogul (Steven Speilberg's son and Kevin Kline & Phoebe Cates in attendance with their daughter) | | Karin Bacon Events |
| 1997 April 18 | *Amazing Tails*: "Camp Gone to the Dogs" | | Animal Planet |
| 1997 April 23 | Japanese Radio Live "Tokyo Today" | | |
| 1997 September 23 | *Good Morning America:* "Animal Intelligence" | | ABC, New York |
| 1998 May | *Dog Fancy* | Magazine | |
| 1999 March 15 | *Dateline NBC:* "Analyze This" | | NBC, New York |
| 1999 May 15 | "Why Dogs Cry & Chimpanzees Cry" (2-hour documentary) | The Discovery Channel | Fleischer Film Documentary People |
| 2002 February 20 | Guilford Rotary Club | | |
| 2002 September 10 | *Reading Rainbow*: "Unsung Heroes" | Lavar Burton | |
| 2002 September | *"Positively Connecticut"* (Reproduction for CPTV) | CT Public Television | Diane Smith |
| 2005 | Boy Scouts of America | Madison, CT | |

| 2006 | *News 8*: "Deaf Dogs" (WTNH CT) | Jocelyn Maminta | ABC, Connecticut |
| --- | --- | --- | --- |
| 1999 - 2006 | Various schools, organizations, churches, expositions such as: <br> * 1st Congregational Church, Clinton <br> * Presbyterian Church, Newark, DE <br> * Methodist Church, Clinton: Children's Sermon <br> * North Madison Congregational Church, Madison: Children's Sermon, Sunday School classes, Christmas pageant, Signing choir's hymn <br> * Senior Clubs <br> * Civic Organizations <br> * Southern CT State University <br> * Killingworth Arts Festivals | | |

# Appendix 2

## Hogan's News Coverage and Publications

| Date | Examples of Written Material | Media | Other Information |
|------|------------------------------|-------|-------------------|
| | *The Register*: Today's Woman | Newspaper | |
| 1994 Summer | PetLife | Newsletter | CT Humane Society |
| 1995 Summer | *Gadzooks!* | Newsletter | Jack Hanna |
| 1995 | Pet Forum | Newsletter | Gina Cadorette |
| 1995 April 11 | *Clinton Recorder* | Newspaper | |
| 1995 September 29 | *Pet Connection* | Journal | |
| 1995 October 2 | *New Haven Register* | Newspaper | |
| 1995 October 8 | *Connecticut Post* | Newspaper | |
| 1995 October 12 | CHETA, *Bits, Bytes & Media* | Professional Journal | |
| 1995 November 15 | *Shoreline Times* | Newspaper | |
| 1995 December 1 | Tail Waggers | Newsletter | |
| 1996 | *Your Dog*, Tufts University | Magazine | |
| 1996 March 5 | *Hartford Courant* | Newspaper | |

| | | | |
|---|---|---|---|
| 1996 March 26 | *Middletown Press* | Newspaper | |
| 1996 May 16 | *The Herald* | Newspaper | |
| 1996 October 1 | *The Source* | Newspaper | |
| 1996 December 6 | *Clinton Recorder* | Newspaper | |
| 1997 Spring | SPCA Today | Newsletter | |
| 1997 January 12 | *New Haven Register: Connecticut* | Newspaper | |
| 1997 January 14 | *Clinton Recorder* | Newspaper | |
| 1997 June 1 | *Dog & Kennel* | Dog Magazine | |
| 1997 September 8 | ADVANCE for Speech-Language Pathologists & Audiologists | Professional Weekly | |
| 1998 May | *Dog Fancy* | Dog Magazine | |
| 1999 | *Dogs Behaving Badly* | Book | Dr. Nicholas Dodman Professor Emeritus, Animal Behaviorist, Tufts University, Boston MA |
| 2001 | *Absolutely Positively Connecticut* | Book | Diane Smith |
| 2002 February 20 | The Guilford Rotarian | Newsletter | |
| 2006 May | *Southern Life* | Newspaper | Southern CT State University |
| 2006 June | *Killingworth Krier* | Newspaper | Chamber of Commerce |
| 2007 February 18 | *New York Times* | Newspaper | Michelle York |

# Appendix 3

## Hogan's ASL Vocabulary

(The words are in alphabetical order after the first
two which were taught in the first 24 hours
after Hogan's adoption.)

1. Sit
2. Cookie
3. Bad
4. Bath
5. Beautiful
6. Bed
7. Bite
8. Boy
9. Bow
10. Bye
11. Calm
12. Car
13. Cat
14. Christmas
15. Come
16. Dance
17. Doctor
18. Down
19. Drop
20. Eat
21. Friend
22. Georgia
23. Girl
24. Go
25. Good
26. Finished/All Gone
27. Handsome
28. Happy
29. Hi
30. Hogan
31. Hug
32. Hungry
33. I Love You
34. Ice Cream
35. In (for returning inside)
36. India
37. Jump
38. Kiss
39. Listen
40. Look
41. Love
42. Mama
43. Medicine
44. No
45. Okay
46. Out (for going outside)
47. Papa
48. Play
49. Please
50. Potty
51. Quiet
52. Run
53. Sad
54. Share
55. Sleep
56. Sing
57. Sorry
58. Stand
59. Stay
60. Thank you
61. Teeth
62. Toy
63. Walk
64. Wake up
65. Want
66. Water
67. What
68. Where
69. Where is Papa/ Mama?
70. Yes
71. You
72. Do you want?
73. No fight

# Appendix 4

## Beginning Letter

Hello! I am so very glad to hear from you. There is so much to say about loving and living with a deaf pup that I can only begin here. What I know for absolute certainty is that I would not trade my life with my deaf pups for anything in the world!

The best advice I can give anyone with a deaf pup, child, friend, or relative is to establish a solid method of communication. Communication is the *key* to success. I didn't know American Sign Language (ASL) before adopting my Hogan, so my husband purchased a pocket-sized book for me to use. I decided to use ASL because I know many folks who comprehend at least a bit of sign. I didn't have to "reinvent the wheel" so to speak. Additionally, when I had to leave my pups with a sitter or the vet, I merely had to give them the handbook or copies of the most important signs that I use. ASL made it possible for many other people to "talk" with my pups without a great deal of instruction which could be vital in sudden situations! Most importantly, my pups were never left in a totally "silent" environment. Someone was always able to talk to them.

I also adopted a deaf female Dalmatian named Georgia. Along with Hogan, Georgia and my hearing black Labrador, India, understood many signs and short sentences. I used over 70 signs with them, and they loved my signing to them. It was wonderful being able to "talk" with them and to have them understand what I was saying. They became quite intent, and folks often commented about how they could see my pups watching my hands and face for messages.

I started through simple repetition. "Sit" is great to start along with "cookie." Once your pup puts together cookie and the reward, you will be off and running! Keep it simple and always use a sign for what you want. Deaf pups are smart and very capable of learning. Because dogs are physical or tactile in nature, they visibly watch for signals and body language.

Since they loved riding in the car, I even taught them the sign for "car." Whenever I told them that we were embarking on a road trip, they ran for the door. "Kiss" was fun and going for a "walk" met with joy-filled approval. "Potty" (I used the sign for toilet which is simply the letter "T") is handy. I signed it every time I took them out to go potty, and they knew I meant business, especially if it was late and I wanted to go to "bed."

I used repetition in training my pups to understand the signs. I simply used the sign for the word and followed it with having them do what I wanted or needed them to do.

Always be gentle, patient, and very positive.

Reward, never punish. The more you reward, the more the pup will respond. I performed all my training with positive reward and reinforcement.

Socialization is also extremely important. It needs to be continuous and endless. Let others give treats which will make meeting other people a wonderful experience for your pup.

Desensitization to scary situations, such as being startled or awakened suddenly, is also critical and needs to be done slowly, carefully, and patiently.

Praise is crucial, touch is essential, and massage works wonders.

AND... Remember that a tired dog is a good dog!

**Our deaf animals can be wonderful and loving members of our families if we remember they have some special needs.**

# Appendix 5

## Tips For Living With
## A Deaf Dog

Written by Connie Bombaci
Edited by Dr. Nicholas Dodman
Posted on Pet Place

*"(There are) none so deaf as those who refuse to hear."*
(Adapted) Matthew Henry, Commentaries, (1708-1710)

*"Who have eyes but do not see, who have ears but do not hear"*
Jeremiah 5:21

A dopting a dog into your family can certainly be an adventure. Diet, training, housebreaking and time are only a few of the considerations. Add deafness to the equation and many run for cover. A cloud of myth too often seems to hover over a dog who is found to be deaf. Some claim that deaf dogs are dumb and unable to learn. Others maintain that they are difficult to train, moody and certain to be hit by cars. On the contrary, deaf dogs are lovable and intelligent animals who have the capacity to bring great joy and companionship into our lives. They are not in pain, nor do they need our pity. They are happy and can be socialized and trained, and like their hearing canine friends, they respond positively and with great affection when given regular and consistent doses of patience, understanding, and praise.

To begin, deafness may be the result of different reasons. Some dogs are born deaf because of their genetic makeup. Other dogs acquire deafness as a result of infection, toxicosis, or old age. A thorough medical examination by a qualified veterinarian is always recommended to determine the cause, the extent, and any possible treatment. Whether the deafness is treatable or not, the bottom line is that your dog is capable of leading a full and enjoyable normal life.

## Deaf Dogs: Communication is the Key to Success

Anyone acquainted with a deaf pup, child, friend, or relative knows well that establishing a solid method of communication is essential. By purchasing a pocket-sized handbook on American Sign Language (ASL), you do not have to know any ASL prior to adopting your deaf pup. ASL is easy to use and convenient for several reasons. There are more people than you might imagine. That makes it possible for other folks to "talk" with your pup. Additionally, when you have to leave your dog with a sitter or the vet, all you have to do is either leave the handbook with marked signs or copies of the most important signs. Your dog will then never be left in a totally "silent" world. Someone will always be able to communicate with your dog without a great deal of instruction, which could prove to be invaluable in the event of any sudden or emergency situations!

## Getting Started with Your Deaf Dog

Start the same way that you would start with a hearing dog—simple repetition, patience, reward, and lots of praise. The only difference in training a deaf dog is that you use your hands instead of the spoken word. Dogs are physical by nature so it will not take long before they begin to watch your hands intently for cues. You should begin with something that is a real attention grabber. "Cookie" is always a puppy pleaser. (Cookie = shape your right hand into the letter "C" and rotate the tips of the fingers on the flat palm of your left hand as if you were cutting out a cookie.) With your dog facing you, make the sign for cookie and then give him a delectable treat. Wait a few seconds and repeat. Once your pup puts together "cookie" and the reward, you will be off and running! Keep it simple and always use a sign for what you want. Before you know it, your dog will watch your hands hoping they will communicate something yummy.

You can follow this by teaching your dog "sit." Remember always to reward and praise, praise, praise. Dogs have learned as many as 65 different signs such as cookie, sit, come, stay, lay down, potty, stop and drop it. They can even learn the signs for their individual names. "Potty" (use the sign for toilet which is simply the letter "T" formed by putting your right thumb between your index and middle fingers and shake slightly) is great for housebreaking and later asking your dog if he needs to go out. Sign it every time you take him out to go potty. Remember always to be gentle, patient and very positive. Reward, never punish. The more you reward, the more the pup will respond. Enrolling in a reputable, basic obedience class is also a great idea. Just use your hands!

## Socialization and Desensitization of Deaf Dogs

All dogs need to be socialized, but socialization is especially important for our deaf dogs. By allowing other people to give your dog treats from a young age, you can ensure that meeting strangers will become a wonderful experience. Desensitization to scary situations such as being startled or awakened suddenly is a must and needs to be done with care, patience, and a slow pace. Practice coming up from behind and touching your dog when he is not looking at you. Wake your dog from sleep by touching the bed or area where he is sleeping or gently patting him. Begin this very gently and increase the motion slowly. This will help to lessen the possibility of your dog being startled by sudden movement or out of a sound sleep.

## Safety is Critical to Deaf Dogs

Providing for your dog's safety is paramount. They cannot hear approaching dangers and need to be kept in secure environments. Fenced in yards are best, and doors to unsupervised or unfenced yards should be kept shut. If you do not have a fenced yard, long leads provide a fun and safe way to exercise your dog in an open area. Harnesses are safest on long leads. When walking your dog, a Gentle Leader® provides the greatest control. The Easy Walk® harness also allows you to lead your dog rather than having him pull on a neck collar.

Both collars/harnesses virtually eliminate the possibility of the collar slipping over the dog's head. Safety collars such as the Martingale® combine a flat collar with a limited tightening feature which also keeps the dog from being able to back out of his collar, becoming free, and being exposed to danger. Be sure to include "DEAF" on your dog's nametag or embroidered on the collar/harness so he will not be misunderstood if he is ever gets lost.

## Recall or Calling Deaf Dogs

Deaf dogs must be able to see you to "hear" you. For this reason, you need to become creative in recalling your dog when his back is towards you. Inside the house, you can stomp on the floor, and your dog will feel the vibration. As soon as he looks at you, motion "come" and reward as soon as he starts to come to you. You can flash a light on and off to call your dog from upstairs, downstairs, outside, or another room. You can even toss a soft toy in his direction to get his attention, and waving your arms catches his peripheral vision. Vibrating collars are also available, but be careful never to get one with the shock feature. At dusk or dark, you can use a flashlight or laser light to recall your dog. Remember to praise and reward every time your dog comes when you call him.

## Exercise and the Deaf Dog

All dogs need good exercise for good health and enjoyment. Deaf dogs are no different and love to run and play. Lure coursing, Frisbee catching, jogging, agility work, and fetching are just a few of the fun things that help them feel active, build confidence, and maintain happiness. Deaf dogs have also been known to bond especially close to their human families. With this special relationship comes the increased risk of separation anxiety whenever their human is not present which makes good aerobic exercise paramount.

## Ten Special Tips for our Special Canine Friends

1. Learn to communicate with them.
2. Always let them know when you are nearby.

3. Always be gentle.
4. Train using lots of praise and other positive reinforcements.
5. Allow them to approach a newcomer first by smelling the person's palm or closed fist.
6. Provide outdoor fencing that is secure and essential for their safety.
7. Work with them in an established and continual training program.
8. Love and accept them with their special needs.
9. Tether them to you in the house in order to help with initial adjustment, housebreaking, bonding, and helping them feel safe.
10. Keep them on leashes and close to you when out on walks. Nametags should include your dog's name and the word "DEAF" in the event he is ever lost so that he is not misunderstood.

## Welcoming a Deaf Canine Friend

Start by putting the "right foot forward" and your mind and heart in the best place possible. Decide from the beginning that success is the only acceptable option, and then plan to do whatever is necessary to ensure that success. The rewards will prove well worth the effort! Adopting any dog takes commitment, love, patience, and understanding. Our deaf dogs are no different. They can be welcomed by us from their world of silence with some simple signs of love.